happiness
fades when it's chased, but
fulfillment
lasts when it's
cultivated.

BILL RYAN

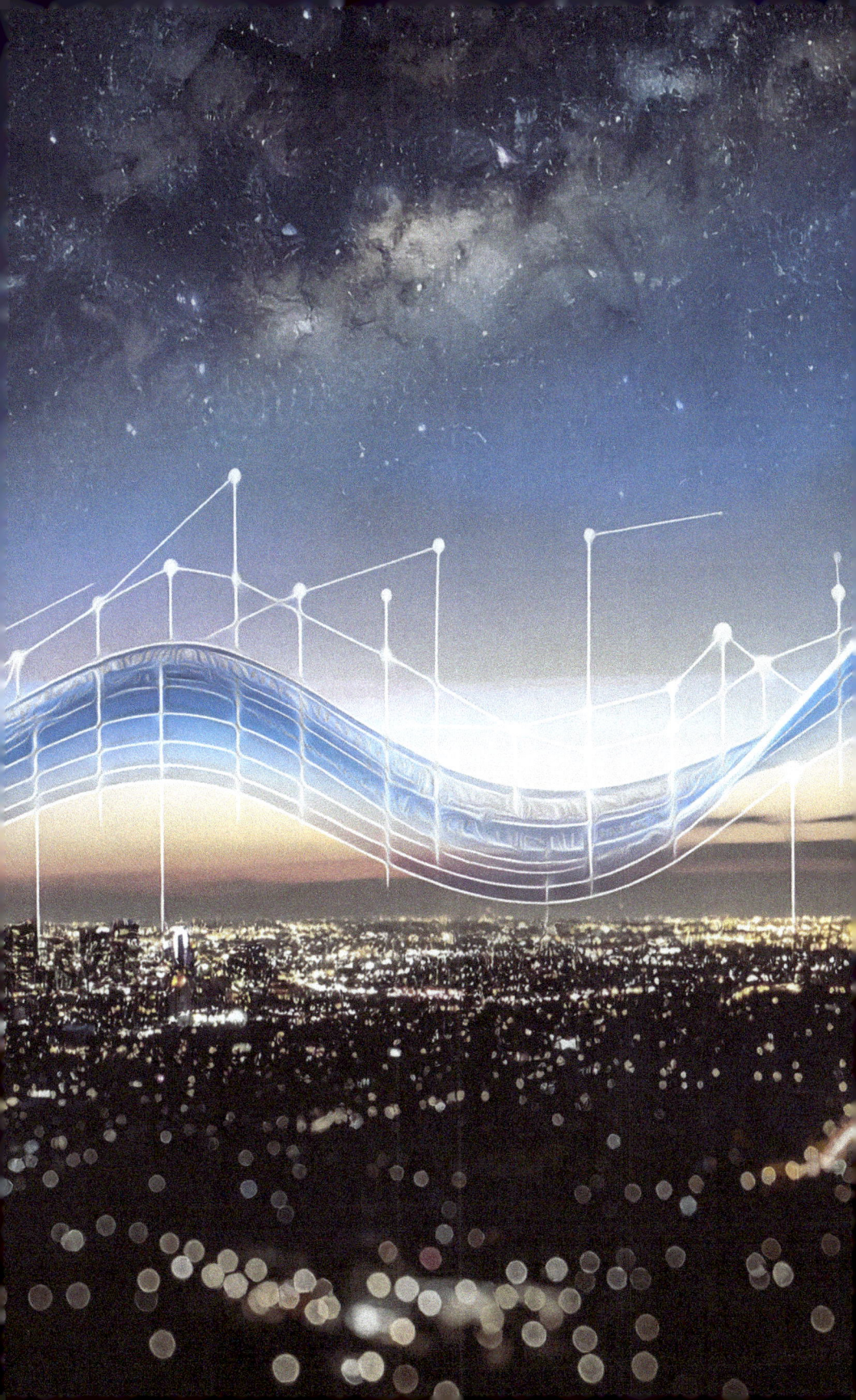

THE
FULFILLMENT
curve

THE
FULFILLMENT
curve

Copyright ©2025 Bill Ryan

Cover Design, Interior Layout and Artwork:
Kris VanderVies | KMDezine Studio, California

This book is a work of nonfiction. All stories and reflections are true to the best of the author's knowledge and experience. Any similarity to persons living or deceased in examples or scenarios is purely coincidental.

Printed in the United States of America.
First Edition.

ISBN: 979-8-9927259-3-3 | HARDCOVER
ISBN: 979-8-9941296-2-3 | PAPERBACK
ISBN: 979-8-9941296-5-4 | PAPERBACK (KDP)
ISBN: 979-8-9941296-0-9 | EBOOK

LIVEFORWARD
PUBLISHING

THE
FULFILLMENT
curve

RECLAIMING PEACE IN A WORLD THAT WANTS MORE

BILL RYAN

Part Two   II   *Understanding Fulfillment* **49**

Chapter 9 | *The Fulfillment Framework* 143

The Conversation that Changed Everything

Friendship has always held a sacred place in my life. I have never needed a crowd—just a few rare souls who elevate the way I experience the world.

This book was born from one of those souls—and from one of those moments.

It began as a quiet conversation with a close friend. We were not trying to be profound. We were simply talking, the way longtime friends do—trying to solve a problem, making sense of where we were in life.

But the conversation deepened. We wandered into the big questions: What drives us? What satisfies us? Why do moments of success sometimes feel strangely hollow?

Then I said something that caught me off guard—something unplanned, but deeply true.

A thread pulled loose. A truth I had not seen until that moment revealed itself: I had spent years chasing—And only now was I beginning to learn how to choose. In that moment, I understood the point of our pursuits.

The pursuit of achievement can resemble a treadmill that never slows down. You keep running, keep pushing, always focused on the next milestone. And when you reach it, there is another. And another. The pace becomes its own reward—until it does not.

I know that treadmill well. I have run on it. I have hit the goals. Built the businesses. Won the accolades. I have made it happen, again and again.

But in that moment of awakening, something shifted. I saw, with startling clarity, that achievement alone is not the measure of a meaningful life. Fulfillment through achievement is where the real depth lies.

Because achievement without alignment—with who you are, what matters to you, and how you want to live—is a hollow pursuit. It is success by someone else's definition. And it will never satisfy the part of you that longs for more than just momentum.

This truth hit even harder a few weeks later.

I was sitting in my home office—whiteboard full of timelines, browser tabs open with investor decks, production updates, and launch schedules for multiple ventures I am building. It looked impressive. And in many ways, it was impressive. But somewhere between my third Zoom meeting and another round of revisions, I caught myself thinking:

What is all this for?

Not in a moment of doubt—but in a moment of awareness. I was not burned out or lost. I was simply awake—aware of how easily motion can masquerade as meaning, and how often we sacrifice clarity in the name of progress.

That is when the truth came full circle: I do not just want to grow—I want to grow with intention. I want to build things that matter. I want success that feels as good on the inside as it looks from the outside.

That is what The Fulfillment Curve is about.

Not the end of achievement—but its evolution. Not slowing down—but going deeper. Not chasing more—but choosing well.

Why "The Fulfillment Curve"?

The title of this book is not just a metaphor—it is a map.

A curve, by nature, implies movement. It rises. It peaks. It changes direction. And so does our experience of fulfillment.

In the early stages of life and career, achievement tends to track upward. We work hard, we reach goals, and we feel the satisfaction that comes with progress. But at a certain point, something shifts. More no longer feels like better. The wins do not land the same. The applause quiets in its ability to move us. We may still be achieving, but we are no longer fulfilled.

THE
FULFILLMENT
curve

That is the essence of the curve: it captures the hidden arc of our striving. It mirrors the law of diminishing returns—not just in economics, but in the human experience. Push too far without reflection, and what once gave us meaning begins to feel hollow.

The Fulfillment Curve is about recognizing that turning point. It is about learning when to keep going—and when to let go. When to build—and when to ask what we are building for. This book invites you to pause at that inflection point and ask the deeper questions. Not to abandon ambition, but to align it. To shift from chasing success to choosing what matters.

Chasing vs. Choosing

We live in a world
that rewards the chase.

From a young age, we are taught to run—to
pursue, to climb, to hustle. We are told that
achievement is the measure of a life well
lived. But achievement, on its own, is a
moving target. It is the next milestone, the
next goal, the next title, the next "success."
The problem is, this pursuit is often
divorced from any real sense of meaning.

We chase because we are conditioned
to chase. But we rarely pause to ask:
What am I chasing? Why? And
what happens when I catch it?

This book is about that pause.

It is about the moment when we stop running long enough to realize that achievement is only part of the equation. True fulfillment requires something deeper. It is not about arriving at a fixed destination—it is about alignment. It is when your goals serve your soul. When the doing reflects your being.

You can still grow. You can still strive. But you will do it from a place of wholeness, not emptiness. This is the shift—from chasing to choosing. From being driven by lack to being led by vision. From climbing a ladder to building a life.

You will learn how to set goals that matter, create systems that serve you, and move through life with both momentum and meaning.

Welcome to

The
Fulfillment
Curve.

The Achievement Trap

THE MOMENTUM THAT MASKS MISALIGNMENT

*Not everyone is wired to crave
high achievement—and
that is more than okay.*

I have come to believe deeply in
honoring each person's path. We
are all here to make our mark
in some way, to leave behind a
quiet echo that says, "I was here."
That is the magic of being alive.

The desire to change the world, to do something meaningful, often starts with a spark of insight. But even the most passionate conviction is still personal. What moves me may not move you—and that is the beauty of it. My job is not to convince, but to follow that call and see where it leads. Maybe, just maybe, it is a noble path—one worth walking.

We each carry a unique voice, a distinct spirit. As a father, that belief shaped how I raised my children. I wanted to give them space—the freedom to chart their own course—and grace, the forgiveness to fall. My role was not to shield them from failure, but to be there when it came. To protect their inner light, not just their outer behavior.

I have never worried much about "bad choices" in good-hearted people. What concerns me more is what dims their spirit—what stifles their potential. That is what I sought to guard.

Life, after all, is not one thing. What feels meaningful to me may not resonate with you—and I love that. I have learned to celebrate that diversity, to stay open to being wrong, because that is how we keep growing.

Who knows where the next great lesson will come from?

Human potential is infinite. So, stay open. Follow what inspires you. And share what you learn along the way.

Part I explores the hidden cost of achievement when it becomes our identity.

It is the steep climb at the beginning of the curve—energizing, impressive, but eventually unsustainable. This is where we confront the dissonance between chasing and choosing.

In *Chapter 1*, we examine how our culture's obsession with success teaches us to tie our worth to movement, to milestones, and to the approval of others.

In *Chapter 2*, we explore how goals we once chose freely can harden into chains—obligations that no longer reflect who we are, but who we used to be.

And in *Chapter 3*, we uncover the myth of arrival: the belief that peace and fulfillment live at the finish line, only to discover that the finish line keeps moving.

These chapters are not about abandoning ambition.

They are about noticing when ambition starts to outrun alignment.

Because before we can begin to define fulfillment, we must first see what we have been using to measure it.

This is where the curve begins.

Not with collapse—but with awakening. Not with giving up—but with the courage to ask a different question. Not just: What's next? But: What matters?

1

CHAPTER ONE

Explore the cultural obsession with
achievement and how it conditions us
to constantly seek the next milestone.

Always Chasing

*W*e live in a culture obsessed
with achievement. It is everywhere—on
our screens, in our conversations, baked
into the very language of success.

Let me ask you: How many of you
reading this right now have a favorite
influencer you follow on social media?

No judgment here. I do too.

But it is worth pausing to ask: What are they
really selling? What version of success are
they modeling? And more importantly—does
their version of "having made it" actually
resonate with who you want to become?

It might even be helpful to chart the messaging that moves you. Take a moment to list what draws you in. Notice the themes. The promises. The polished images of a perfect life.

Then, as you move through this book, revisit that chart. You may find that what once inspired you now feels hollow. Or maybe you will realize you have been chasing something that was never actually yours to want.

You see, our culture is not just supportive of achievement—it is obsessed with it.

I say this not from a place of judgment, but from experience.

My first book—"Fix Your Why"—was achievement-driven too. I deliberately used the word *achievement* to avoid the word *success*. Success felt loaded, tangled with expectations and image. Achievement seemed cleaner. But if I am transparent, I was not just parsing words.

I was still chasing.

That is why I am writing this book.

The Fulfillment Curve is where the chase slows down. Where the language shifts. Where meaning starts to take shape.

The Pursuit That Never Ends

There is a story I have heard—and maybe you have too. A man spends years working to become a partner at his firm. He puts in the hours, sacrifices weekends, misses dinners, and bypasses vacations. One day, it happens—he gets the title, the corner office, the bigger paycheck. He pops the champagne, maybe even sheds a tear of pride.

But a week later, he feels...off. Not depressed, exactly. Not ungrateful. Just… empty.

He wonders, Is this it?

That man could be any of us.

While this story chronicles a chapter in a life, the lesson it teaches applies to each day we live. We can spend a career pursuing a "measure" of achievement and look back with regret.

We think fulfillment lies at the next milestone, but when we get there, it slips away. It is not just a career story—it is a pattern we live out every day.

The Stepping-Stone Mindset

We have all heard the advice to "be present." It has become a kind of spiritual shorthand. But presence is not just a nice idea—it is *where fulfillment actually lives.*

The problem is, many of us do not really live in the present. We endure it. We treat today like a means to an end—a stepping stone to something better. We tell ourselves that once we reach that goal, that number, that recognition, then we will finally feel full.

But fulfillment is not a future reward. It is a present practice.

Presence is where **FULFILLMENT** actually lives.

If you want to know whether you are chasing or choosing, try asking yourself one simple question at the end of each day: Did I treat today like it mattered—or just a stepping stone to something else?

If you rushed through, postponed joy, or told yourself "This does not count yet," you were chasing. And the irony is—when we dismiss the present in pursuit of fulfillment, we disconnect from the only place it can actually happen.

That is why presence matters. Not as a spiritual performance, but as an honest reflection of your values. We say we are choosing fulfillment—but are our actions aligned? Are we really here, or just sprinting toward a future that keeps moving?

Fulfillment begins the moment we stop stepping over the moment we are in.

The Power of Less

When we are caught in the chase, we think the answer is to do more. Push harder. Strive further. But sometimes, the answer is the opposite.

You may feel confused on your path. You have been told to follow your passion, but the way is not clear. You get frustrated, maybe even think about giving up.

Don't.

In those moments of frustration, it might serve you to do less. Expect less. Demand less.

That moment of less might invite the clarity you have been craving.

Early in my career, when pressure mounted and the answers were not coming, I learned to stop. I would walk away from the activity, the deadline, the noise. I created space for the solution to appear.

That moment of less, brought clarity by reducing clutter.

The mind is an incredible instrument—but it will run on autopilot if we let it. When we slow down, when we reconnect to the present, we reclaim our awareness. And from that awareness, fulfillment begins to grow.

The Myth of Arrival

We have been sold an idea that life works like this:

Set a goal → Work hard → Achieve it → Feel fulfilled

It sounds logical. Linear. Fair.

Put in the effort, and the reward will come—not just in outcomes, but in how you feel.

But for many, that last part never fully lands. Or if it does, it fades quickly. We reach a milestone and immediately set another. We do not arrive—we reset.

This is the ***arrival fallacy:*** the belief that happiness, peace, or fulfillment will magically appear once we get there—wherever "there" is.

But "there" is slippery. Vague. Always just a little further away.

We tell ourselves that the next achievement will be the one that makes it all worth it. But when we get there, the high is fleeting—and the hunger returns.

But the goalposts move. Every time.

The danger of the Myth of Arrival is not just that it is false—it is that it is subtle. You can spend decades chasing, achieving, resetting the bar, and chasing again—only to wake up one day and realize that the dream you have been running toward never actually belonged to you.

Fulfillment was not waiting at the finish line. It was waiting for you to stop running.

WORK HARD

SET A GOAL

FEEL FULFILLED

ACHIEVE IT

This is the *Arrival Fallacy:* the belief
that happiness, peace, or fulfillment
will magically appear once we get
there—wherever "there" is.

The Language of Chasing

Look at the words we use when we talk about success:

- Crush your goals.
- Grind until you make it.
- Hustle harder.
- Sleep when you're dead.

These are not the words of a fulfilled person. They are the words of someone running from something—or chasing something they have never defined.

We are surrounded by messaging that reinforces *Chasing*.

It is in the ads that tell us we are one product away from feeling better.

It is in the social media feeds that celebrate hustle, highlight reels, and endless optimization.

It is in the cultural script that equates busyness with value, and achievement with identity.

We are told to go harder, scale faster, do more.

- "Don't stop."
- "Don't settle."
- "Keep climbing."

And if we dare to pause—to breathe, reflect, or ask, "Is this even what I want?"—we are made to feel like we are falling behind.

We have listened to the life coaches: *Put down your phone. Be present. Stay grounded.* And we nod in agreement while scrolling through another highlight reel.

We joke about FOMO—as if naming it makes it harmless.

But beneath the jokes is a deeper truth: We are not just afraid of missing out. We are afraid that if we stop watching, striving, or chasing… we will fall behind. That we will lose relevance. That we will miss the moment.

Ironically, that fear pulls us out of the only moment that is real—this one.

We do not suffer from a lack of information. We suffer from a lack of integration.

We know we need to slow down—but we do not know how to stop performing long enough to be still.

Why We Chase

Why do we do it?

Why do we keep chasing—more money, more status, more recognition—even when something inside us whispers, "This is not it?"

There are a few deep-rooted reasons we get stuck in the chase:

1. *Validation Addiction:* External success gives us feedback: applause, money, approval. It feels good—for a while. But it fades, so we chase it again.

2. *Cultural Conditioning:* We are taught to equate busyness with value. The more we do, the more we are worth. Stillness is mistaken for laziness. Reflection is seen as indulgence.

3. *Fear of Enough:* If we stop striving, we fear we will fall behind—or worse, become irrelevant. "Enough" feels like settling. So, we keep moving, often without knowing where we are going.

But the truth is, sometimes the chase is not even ours. Sometimes, we inherit it.

curve

The Patterns We Inherit

Many of us grew up watching the people who raised us—especially our fathers—caught in their own chase. Chasing status. Control. Security. They believed that if they could just provide enough, prove enough, accomplish enough… it would all be worth it.

We, as children, saw it differently. We saw the toll it took. The absence in the name of providing. The tension beneath the roof. The long hours and the silence that followed.

And all we really wanted… was their presence.

Some of us told ourselves we would do it differently.

- We would be more balanced.
- More present.
- More free.

But the patterns live in us like muscle memory.

Chasing becomes our default—not because we want the same things, but because no one ever showed us another way.

And so we run, just like they did.

But somewhere inside, we wonder: What if we stopped? What if we broke the pattern? What if success did not have to look like sacrifice?

It is amazing—the messages we send ourselves that are not received. There is a voice inside, quiet but persistent, that whispers: "This is not it." A deep knowing that the running will not deliver what we hope it will—that fulfillment does not live at the end of the chase.

And yet… we still run.

We run out of habit. Out of fear. Out of identity that has been shaped by motion and momentum. Sometimes we run not because we believe there is something better ahead, but because we do not know how to be still where we are.

...not because we want the same things, but because **no one ever showed us another way.**

That is the paradox at the center of the human experience—the part of us that "knows" better, and the part that keeps running anyway.

My Moment of Reckoning

I know this pattern well. In 1987, I was deep in it.

I had taken on an ambitious project: building a 5,000-square-foot custom home for the Parade of Homes. But I entered late, which meant I had to compress months of work into weeks.

Every day was a scramble. I was on-site constantly, coordinating trades, solving problems, begging contractors to work side by side, asking the impossible just to keep the project moving.

It was not just a house—it was a statement. A chance to prove something. To be seen. To matter.

When no one would take on the hardwood floors under my timeline, I bought a sander and did it myself.

That night, I worked alone past 4 a.m., hands stained, eyes half-open, body exhausted. And driving home in the dark, it hit me: I was succeeding. I was delivering. I was "winning."

And I was empty.

In that moment, I realized: *I had confused movement for meaning.* I had said yes to pressure so many times, I no longer knew how to say yes to peace.

That night was not a grand awakening. It was not a breakdown or a breakthrough. It was something quieter—a reckoning.

I saw how easily we get pulled into this cycle. Not overnight, but inch by inch. Until busyness becomes who we are. Until peace feels like a stranger.

And in the stillness of that dark road, a voice inside me finally spoke—not loudly, but clearly: "This is not it."

The Choice

That voice was familiar. It sounded like the boy I once was—the one who just wanted more time with his father.

And now, with a second child on the way, I stood at a crossroads.

Would I keep running, like so many men before me?

Would I keep proving, keep producing, thinking I could outrun the emptiness?

Or would I stop? Would I break the pattern? Would I become the father I once longed for?

That night, I made a choice. Not a dramatic one. Not a forever one. But enough.

Enough to realize that fulfillment is not earned through exhaustion. It is protected through presence.

That night was the beginning of something new—a new rhythm, a new lens, a new way of living.

It was not the end of the chase. But it was the first step toward choosing something better.

The High Cost of the Chase

Chasing has a price—and it is not just time and energy.

It costs us pieces of ourselves.

The longer we stay in pursuit, the more we shape-shift to match the path we are on. We start to confuse who we are with what we are achieving. The proving becomes the point. And somewhere along the way, we forget the version of ourselves that existed before the chase began.

It strains our relationships, too. We say things like, "I'll be present once I finish this project," or "It's just a season." But the season never ends. The finish line keeps moving. And the people waiting for us begin to fade—until we no longer remember how to slow down long enough to really be with them. Or with ourselves.

It also numbs our capacity for joy. Even when something good happens, we barely feel it. There is no pause. No breath. No celebration. Just a quick glance before we set our sights on the next thing.

That is the trap of the chase: It keeps us future-focused. But fulfillment only happens in the now.

And that is the paradox.

Eyes locked on the horizon might be fine for driving a car—but it is a disorienting way to live a life. Because when you are always reaching for what is next, you miss what is here. You miss the people beside you. You miss yourself.

Fulfillment does not wait at the end of the road. It is in your hands.

Right here.

Right now.

The Shift Begins With Awareness

If you have ever felt empty after a win—reached the goal, crossed the finish line, held the trophy, and thought, "Is this all?"—you are not alone.

And more importantly, you are not broken.

You are simply standing at the edge of a shift. A shift most people will feel at some point—but not everyone will honor.

It is the shift from chasing to choosing. From seeking to seeing. From achievement as identity to achievement as a tool—a means, not the meaning.

This shift does not crash in. It arrives quietly. A flicker of unease after the victory. A whisper of doubt in a moment that should have felt like enough.

But that flicker? It is sacred. It is the moment the autopilot starts to fail. The beginning of a deeper knowing: that something about your trajectory needs to change.

That is when the curve begins.

Not a crash. Not a leap. A gentle bend in direction. From outward pressure to inward clarity. From doing more to being more present. From striving to choosing.

It starts with awareness. And from there, everything can change. You can change.

Not someday. Not when you finally arrive. With the very next choice, you begin bending your life toward meaning.

Toward peace over pressure. Presence over performance. Values over velocity.

You do not need a grand declaration. Just one real decision—followed by another, and another. That is how the Fulfillment Curve begins to form.

It is not a destination. It is a way of living. A quiet, courageous turn toward what matters most.

And it starts right now.

The Curve vs. The Climb

Sustained Fulfillment or Endless Striving—Which Path Will You Choose?

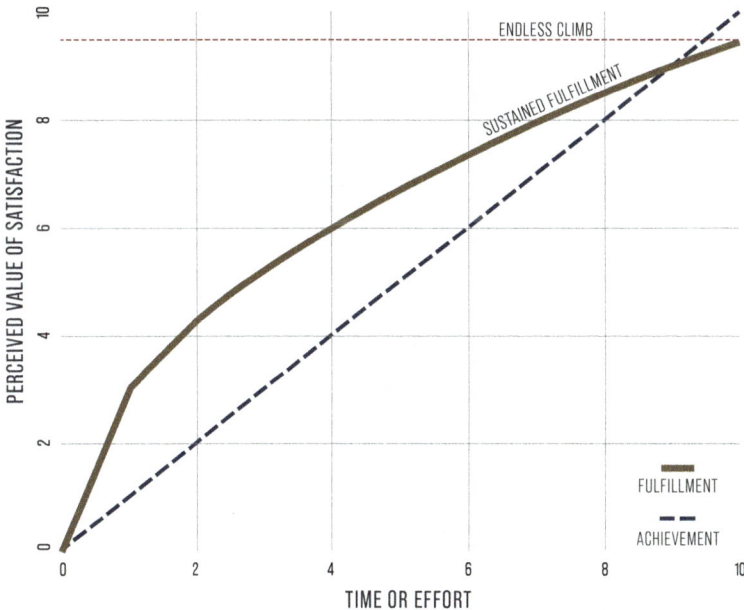

The Fulfillment Curve (bold line):
A graceful bend—steep at first, but gradually leveling into sustained satisfaction, intention, and presence.

The Achievement Climb (dashed line):
A relentless upward climb—linear, demanding, and often unsustainable.

Reflection Prompts

Chasing achievement is often rewarded. But rarely questioned. We set goals, reach them, and move the bar again—faster, higher, more. Until one day, something does not feel right. The win does not land. The moment does not satisfy. And we are left wondering why.

That wondering is where truth begins.

If you have ever felt the hollow after the high, you're not alone. It does not mean you failed. It means you are awake. And now, you have a choice: to keep running... or to turn inward. Start here:

- When was the last time I reached a goal but still felt unsatisfied?
- What am I chasing today—and do I know why?
- If I stopped chasing, what might I discover instead?

This is not the end of ambition. It is the beginning of alignment. Let these questions open a space within you—one where fulfillment can finally find its way in.

Closing Thought

There is nothing wrong with ambition. Ambition builds. It stretches. It creates. But unchecked, it becomes a treadmill—always running, never arriving.

The real question is not just "What are you chasing?" The deeper question is: "What do you want to feel?"

And even deeper still: "Can you choose that now? Not someday. Not "when things settle." Not after you have earned it.

Because if what you truly want is peace, or purpose, or joy—then the chase may only delay it. But the choice... brings it within reach.

This is the invitation of the Fulfillment Curve: To stop postponing your life. To begin living it.

The Curve
vs.
The Climb

There are two ways to orient a life.

The first is the path of achievement—upward, constant, urgent. This is the *Achievement Climb*. It is what we are sold by culture: more is better. Success is linear. If you keep climbing, fulfillment will meet you at the top.

But that climb rarely delivers what it promises. The higher you go, the farther the finish line moves. And even when you reach it, the moment is fleeting. A breath, then another summit to chase.

The second path is quieter—but more honest. It is the *Fulfillment Curve*. It begins with movement and ambition too, but something shifts. You start listening inward. You begin to value how it feels, not just how it looks. And slowly, the trajectory changes. The path bends. You no longer need to climb for the sake of climbing.

Fulfillment is not about stopping—it is about realigning. The pace slows, but the richness deepens.

This curve matters.

Not a destination, but a way of being. Not a trophy, but a truth.

The moment you stop chasing and start choosing, you are already on it.

2

How even worthy goals can
become prisons when they are
disconnected from deeper values.

When Goals
Become Chains

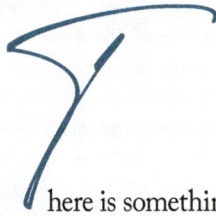

here is something sacred about
setting a goal. It means we believe in
our own potential. It signals hope—that
we are capable of something more.

In those early moments, dreams feel
weightless—like they float just ahead of us,
pulling us forward with energy and clarity.
They reflect the best of who we are and who
we hope to become. They give structure to
our ambition and meaning to our motion. It
is the beginning of the upward curve, where
momentum and meaning feel aligned.

But what happens when the goals we once set with joy and clarity begin to feel like obligations? What happens when we are no longer pulled by passion, but pushed by pressure?

Dreams do not always stay light. Somewhere along the climb, what once felt expansive begins to constrict. The joy fades.

That is when goals become chains.

And yet, we often do not notice the shift. We keep grinding, thinking we are being disciplined or resilient, when in truth we are just afraid to let go. Afraid of being seen as a quitter. Afraid of disappointing others—or worse, ourselves. The dream becomes a duty. The vision becomes a verdict. We do not choose it anymore—we serve it.

The irony is that the very goals meant to liberate us can slowly imprison us if we do not stay awake to why we are chasing them in the first place.

Fulfillment does not live in the relentless pursuit of any goal. It lives in the quiet alignment between who you are and what you are moving toward.

And when a goal no longer serves that alignment, the wise choice is not to push harder—it is to pause, listen, and choose again.

From Freedom to Prison

Not all prisons have bars.

Some are built from the inside out—constructed not by others, but by the ambitions we once embraced. Sometimes, they look like perfectly curated to-do lists, color-coded calendars, and ten-year plans. We call it structure. We call it hustle. But beneath the polish, we may find something more hollow.

We mistake discipline for purpose. We confuse motion for meaning. We wear productivity like armor, afraid of what we might feel if we ever stopped moving.

And before we know it, we are not creating our lives—we are serving our goals. They become our masters, not our mirrors.

We whisper to ourselves, I cannot stop now—I have come this far. Or worse, If I quit, I will be a failure.

But what if continuing is the real failure?

What if the true mistake is not in walking away, but in clinging to a version of success that no longer fits who we are? What if our devotion to the path blinds us to the truth that we have outgrown it?

This is the hidden cost of unchecked ambition. When we forget to check in with ourselves—when we chase without pausing to ask why—we risk becoming prisoners of our own potential.

Freedom is not the absence of effort. It is the presence of choice. And choosing again—especially when it costs us pride or reputation—is sometimes the most courageous thing we can do.

The Inheritance of Old Goals

Does the path still fit the person?

Some of the goals we are chasing today were set by a version of ourselves that no longer exists.

- That twenty-something dream of a corner office.
- That thirty-something vision of a picture-perfect family.
- That revenue target.
- That follower count.
- That title.

At the time, they made sense. But we evolve. And when we do not update our goals to match who we have become, we start living a life that is out of sync with our soul.

Old goals become outdated maps. Following them too long leads us nowhere.

And like any good map, a goal is only useful if it reflects the terrain you are actually walking. What worked when you were twenty-five might not make sense at forty. But we rarely pause long enough to ask if the path still fits the person. Instead, we double down. We push harder. We keep walking, even as our inner compass whispers that we are lost.

This is the quiet burden of inherited goals—they do not just linger; they shape the architecture of our lives long after they have expired. We build careers, relationships, and entire identities around objectives that once gave us purpose but now quietly drain it. And because those goals were once so important to us, it feels like betrayal to question them. We confuse loyalty to our past self with loyalty to our present fulfillment.

But here is the truth: A goal is not a promise you made to the world. It is a tool you once chose to serve you. When it no longer serves, you are not obligated to carry it.

The irony is that we treat these old goals like heirlooms— something precious we must protect—when in reality, they are more like outdated software running in the background, slowing everything down.

The real act of courage is not in achieving the goal. It is in revisiting it. Asking: Do I even want this anymore? And if the answer is no, having the self-respect to let it go without guilt or apology.

This is one of the essential shifts on the Fulfillment Curve—moving from inherited ambition to intentional desire. Not because you have quit. But because you have grown.

On the Fulfillment Curve, this is the point of inflection. The upward slope of drive and discipline begins to turn—not because we have failed, but because we have grown. The question is: Will we notice the turn, or will we keep climbing a hill that no longer leads us home?

Letting Go of Old Maps

Take a moment and list three goals you are currently chasing or holding onto. They might be professional, personal, financial, or even social (like status, recognition, or approval).

For each goal, ask yourself:

- When did I first set this goal?
- What version of me wanted this—and why?
- Does this goal still reflect who I am today?
- If I were starting fresh, would I choose this goal again?

If the answer is no—do not judge yourself. Just notice it. Then, write down one small action you could take to release or revise that goal.

Fulfillment often begins not with chasing something new, but with the willingness to let go of something old.

The Ego Trap

There is a part of us that clings to goals not because they still serve us—but because they have become part of who we think we are.

- "If I let go of this, who am I?"
- "If I stop chasing this, does that mean I failed?"

The ego does not crave growth. It craves recognition. It wants to prove something.

But fulfillment does not come from proving. It comes from *becoming*. And becoming requires release.

Letting go of a goal that no longer fits is not a sign of weakness—it is a sign of wisdom. It is not failure. It is *freedom*.

The ego is a master of disguise. It dresses up fear as ambition. It calls attachment "discipline." It whispers that our worth is measured by how hard we grind. It tells us that quitting means we have lost, when in fact, it might be the first step toward finding ourselves.

Because often, the ego is not fighting for your future. It is fighting to preserve a version of you that has already expired.

That is the trap.

The more tightly we cling to the story we have told ourselves—the title, the image, the external validation—the harder it becomes to hear the quieter voice underneath: The voice of growth. ***The voice of enough.***

Fulfillment begins the moment we stop performing for the imaginary audience in our mind… and start listening to the person we are becoming.

Because the truth is, holding onto an outdated goal to protect your ego is not strength—it is *self-abandonment*.

And the more energy you spend maintaining a version of yourself you have outgrown, the less energy you have **to become who you are meant to be next.**

This is the pivot point on the Fulfillment Curve:

- When you stop performing and start aligning.
- When you stop proving and start *living*.

The Signs Your Goals Are No Longer Serving You

There is a subtle heaviness that creeps in when a goal has outlived its purpose. It does not announce itself loudly. Instead, it shows up in the quiet spaces—when you drag yourself out of bed, when you check off another achievement but feel nothing inside, when you avoid stillness because you are afraid of what you will hear. These are the signs we rarely talk about. Because admitting that a goal no longer serves us feels like weakness—feels like quitting. But the truth is, recognizing when a goal has expired is not failure—it is wisdom.

Is this you:

- You dread the work but fear the alternative.
- You are succeeding, but it does not feel like success.
- You feel disconnected from the reason you started.
- You avoid reflecting because you might not like the answers.

Most of us are trained to muscle through discomfort. To interpret resistance as something to overcome, rather than something to listen to. But not all friction is productive. Sometimes, it is a signal that you have grown beyond the goal itself.

When you dread the work but fear the alternative, it is not laziness—it is misalignment.

When you succeed and feel nothing, it is not ingratitude—it is disconnection.

When you avoid reflection, it is not because you are weak—it is because some part of you already knows the truth.

These moments are not signs that you are broken. They are signs that it is time to pause and re-evaluate. The Fulfillment Curve is not about quitting when things get hard; it is about recognizing when the goal itself is no longer worth the cost.

Your goals should challenge you—but they should not hollow you out.

The question is not: Can I keep going? The question is: Is this still worth pursuing?

Listening to the Signs

Take a few minutes to get honest with yourself. Review the following questions and write down what surfaces without censoring or justifying:

- Is there an area of my life where I feel like I am going through the motions? *(Be specific—career, relationship, personal goal, etc.)*
- What part of the work or pursuit feels heavy or draining right now?
- If I stopped chasing this goal today, what would I gain? What would I lose?

What is one small step I could take this week to explore whether this goal still serves me? (This could be a conversation, journaling session, or simply allowing yourself space to imagine another path.)

Sometimes the most courageous act is not to push forward, but to pause and listen.

Permission to Change Your Mind

You are allowed to change the plan. Not because you are flaky. Not because you are giving up. But because you are growing.

You are allowed to evolve beyond your own expectations.

To outgrow the dreams you once held sacred.

To realize that the version of success you once pursued was shaped by who you were—not who you have become.

You are allowed to say, *"This goal no longer aligns with who I am."* And mean it—not as an excuse, but as an act of self-honesty.

The world teaches us to finish what we start. To power through. To wear endurance as a badge of honor. But there is a deeper wisdom that asks something else:

Finish what still matters.
Let go of what does not.

Because persistence without reflection becomes stubbornness. And discipline without discernment turns into self-denial.

Changing your mind is not failure. It is fidelity—to truth, to growth, to who you are becoming. It is one of the hardest things to do in a world that worships certainty. But the Fulfillment Curve invites us to shift from blind completion to conscious alignment.

Not all goals are meant to be finished.

Some are meant to lead us to the edge of who we were—so we can take the next step as someone new.

A New Way to Set Goals

In the achievement-driven world we have inherited, goals are often treated like trophies—meant to impress, to accumulate, to prove. But the Fulfillment Curve invites a different approach: One that favors alignment over applause. Meaning over momentum. Truth over trend.

And believe me, I know about setting goals.

I am a goal setter—*always* have been.

I have built businesses, chased metrics, mapped out visions with precision. But over time, I have learned that not all goals are created equal. Some move you forward. Others just keep you busy. Some grow from your values. Others grow from your ego.

So, before you set your next one, pause. Ask yourself three questions:

- **Does this goal reflect who I am now?**

  Not who I was when I first imagined it. Not who others expect me to be. But who I am today—with all the clarity, experience, and self-awareness I have earned.

- **Is this goal in service of my values—or just my vanity?**

  Is it rooted in what matters to me—or what looks good from the outside? Am I chasing this because it is right for my soul… or just impressive on a résumé?

- **If I achieved this, would it bring real satisfaction—or just relief?**

  Would I feel grounded, whole, and fulfilled? Or simply less anxious, less behind, less inadequate?

These are not easy questions. But fulfillment does not come from easy answers. It comes from *honest ones*.

If the answer to any of these is "no,"

It is not failure. It is feedback.

And that feedback is an invitation—to pause, to pivot, and to recalibrate.

Because goals should not be monuments to our past selves. They should be pathways to our most aligned future.

Not every mountain is worth the climb.

Reflection Prompts

Not all goals deserve to be carried forward. Some were inherited. Some were fear-born. Some were set by a version of you that no longer exists.

But quitting has been branded a failure. So, we keep going, even when the goal is no longer alive in us. Even when the cost is clarity, energy, and peace.

This is your invitation to pause—not to give up, but to give yourself back.

Ask gently. Listen honestly.

- What goal am I holding onto because I'm afraid to quit?
- Which of my goals were set by someone I no longer am?
- What would freedom look like in this area of my life?

This is not about walking away from everything. It's about returning to what still matters—and letting the rest go.

Closing Thought

Goals should guide us, not govern us. They are tools, not truths. Markers of direction—not definitions of identity.

At their best, goals serve our becoming. But when we begin to serve them—blindly, dutifully, fearfully—they stop being instruments of growth and become instruments of pressure.

If your goals have become chains, it is time to break them. Not out of weakness. Not out of failure. But because something deeper in you has shifted.

You are not on the same curve **anymore.**

What once felt like a climb toward truth may now feel like a loop of obligation. A performance. A ritual without meaning. You are not moving closer—you are circling.

That is the moment to pause.

To stop asking, *"How do I get there?"* And start asking, *"Is that still where I want to go?"*

This is the quiet pivot at the heart of The Fulfillment Curve: The courage to choose again. With open eyes. With a grounded heart. With intent that is not inherited, but owned.

Because real fulfillment does not come from arriving at a goal. It comes from aligning with your truth—again and again, as you evolve.

And that is not giving up.

That is finally showing up—for the life that is actually yours.

The Goal Setter's Confession

I have been setting goals my whole life.

Big ones.

Measurable ones.

Vision-board-worthy ones.

I have mapped them out on spreadsheets, tracked them in journals, stacked them like stepping stones to some imagined summit.

And for a long time, it worked. It gave me direction.

Discipline.

Drive.

But eventually, I noticed something unsettling:

Some goals were not pulling me forward. They were holding me back.

They were not about who I was becoming. They were about who I was afraid to stop being.

I kept chasing them out of habit, out of pride, out of fear that changing course meant failure. But the truth was clearer—and harder to admit:

Not every goal deserves to be finished. Not every mountain is worth the climb. And sometimes, the bravest thing you can do is stop.

Not because you have lost your ambition— But because you have found your alignment.

C H A P T E R   T H R E E

Why achieving something
does not always make us feel
better or more fulfilled.

3

The Illusion of Arrival

"When I get there…"

We have all said it.

"When I get the promotion,
then I'll be happy." "Once I hit that
income level, then I'll relax." "After I find
the right partner, lose the weight, launch
the business—then life will feel right."

This is the *arrival fantasy*—the
belief that fulfillment is just one goal
away. It gives us comfort. It keeps us
moving. But it is a mirage. And the
closer we get, the more it moves.

THE FULFILLMENT curve

The illusion is not just that the goal will satisfy us—it is that it will *complete* us. That once we get "there," we will finally feel at peace, at home in our own lives.

But here is the truth: *There* is a moving target. And more often than not, when we arrive, we barely stop to notice. We raise the bar. We set the next milestone. We trade one finish line for another, and call it progress.

The real trap of the arrival fantasy is not ambition—it is postponement. We keep deferring presence, peace, and joy to a future version of ourselves. We outsource contentment to a someday that never quite arrives.

And the cost?

We live in delay. We work hard, but do not feel whole. We chase success but miss satisfaction. We accomplish, but never quite *arrive*.

This chapter is about recognizing the pattern—and choosing a different path. It is about learning to live *on the curve*, not at the destination. Because fulfillment is not found in arrival. It is found in *alignment*.

Why Arrival Never Feels Like Arrival

When you finally reach the goal you have worked so hard for, something surprising often happens: It does not feel like you thought it would.

- The applause is brief.
- The high fades quickly.
- And the void you were trying to fill? Still there.

You check the box, maybe even celebrate for a moment. But deep down, there is a quiet disappointment. Not because the achievement was not meaningful—but because it did not deliver the *transformation* you were banking on.

You are still you.

The version of yourself who crossed the finish line is the same one who started the race—just with more miles behind you. And so the question emerges: *Was I running toward something real... or just running from discomfort?*

This is not because your goal was wrong. Ambition is not the enemy.

It is because you were expecting the goal to do something it cannot do: **Complete you.**

That is the hidden promise baked into so many of our pursuits:

"If I get there, **I'll finally be enough.**"
"If I achieve that, **I'll finally feel secure.**"
"If I win this, **I'll finally be worthy of rest.**"

But no external win can resolve an internal need for wholeness. And when we ask outcomes to give us identity, they always come up short.

This is why so many high-achievers feel hollow at the top. Why even the most celebrated victories can feel strangely anticlimactic.

Because arrival does not deliver *being*. It only delivers *proof of doing*.

And doing, no matter how impressive, cannot substitute for *belonging to yourself*.

The Dopamine Rollercoaster

Neurologically, achievement gives us a hit of dopamine. It is the brain's chemical reward for progress—a surge of motivation, energy, and pleasure. And it feels amazing... momentarily.

But our brains adapt quickly. What was once thrilling becomes familiar. And what becomes familiar becomes insufficient.

This is called **hedonic adaptation**—the psychological treadmill that ensures today's high becomes tomorrow's baseline. You close the deal. Launch the business. Cross the finish line. And for a fleeting moment, you are flying.

But then the baseline resets. The applause fades. The inbox refills. And you find yourself thinking: *What's next?*

So, we move the bar.

Raise the stakes.

Chase the next hit.

And on and on it goes.

This is not weakness. It is wiring. Our brains are designed to seek novelty and reward. But left unchecked, that drive becomes a trap—a loop of endless striving, where fulfillment is always just out of reach.

We begin mistaking stimulation for satisfaction. Momentum for meaning. Dopamine for depth.

And because each new "high" is followed by an inevitable "low," we learn to live in pursuit, not presence. We convince ourselves that rest is indulgent and stillness is stagnation. We tell ourselves we are building something—but what we are really building is dependency on the *next thing* to feel alive.

This is the rollercoaster of modern ambition: Always climbing, always craving, never arriving.

But fulfillment does not live at the top of the next peak. It lives in stepping off the ride long enough to ask:

What am I really chasing? And why do I believe I need to earn my worth through motion?

Because until we learn to regulate our reward systems with awareness, we will always be ruled by them.

Chasing as a Form of Avoidance

Here is a hard truth: Sometimes we chase goals not to feel fulfilled—but to avoid feeling unfulfilled.

We become experts in productivity—and strangers to purpose.

The pursuit becomes a distraction. As long as we are busy striving, we do not have to sit with the silence. We do not have to face the deeper discomfort that lives beneath all the noise.

Because stillness—real stillness—asks uncomfortable questions:

- What do I really want?
- Is this life aligned with who I am—or just what I have been told to pursue?
- Am I building a life of meaning… or just maintaining momentum?
- Is this path my own—or someone else's version of success I never questioned?

And so we run. And call it ambition.

We hide in motion. Because motion gives us the illusion of progress—even if we are heading in the wrong direction. And as long as there is a goal on the horizon, we can avoid the hollow feeling that maybe... we have lost touch with our *why*.

This is the paradox of high performers: The more capable we are of chasing big goals, the easier it becomes to use achievement as avoidance.

We become experts in productivity—and strangers to purpose.

We fill our calendars, check the boxes, and climb the ladders... All while dodging the fundamental question:

What is this all for?

Because to pause long enough to answer that question would mean confronting what we have ignored: That despite the success, we still feel restless. That under the drive, there is doubt. And that maybe—just maybe—fulfillment requires subtraction, not addition.

But that kind of clarity only comes when we stop running long enough to listen.

To face the silence.

To stop chasing—and start choosing.

Redefining What It Means to "Arrive"

What if arrival is not a destination—but a decision?

What if fulfillment is not something you earn by climbing high enough, fast enough, far enough—but something you access by turning inward, right where you are?

What if the whole paradigm is backwards?

We are conditioned to believe that peace is the prize—that once we "make it," then we can rest. Then we can slow down. Then we can finally be enough.

But what if peace is not the result of success—what if it is the *foundation* of it?

What if true success—the kind that sustains, satisfies, and heals— can only emerge when we stop chasing from lack and start choosing from wholeness?

Because here is the truth: The most meaningful forms of arrival are not marked by fanfare or milestones. They happen quietly—often invisibly—when you come back to yourself.

When you stop outsourcing your worth to metrics and milestones. When you stop running and start listening. When you look at your life, not through the lens of "what's missing," but through the clarity of "what matters."

That is arrival.

It is not a mountaintop moment. It is a posture of presence.

And it is not one and done.

You arrive—not once—but *again and again.*

Each time you say no to a misaligned yes. Each time you pause instead of perform. Each time you choose integrity over image, depth over dopamine, stillness over status.

This is the real shift: From chasing to choosing. From striving to settling *in.* From waiting to live… to living now.

To redefine arrival is to reclaim your timeline.

To step off the treadmill.

To remember that you are not late. You are not behind. You are not broken.

You are here.

And *here* is where the curve begins to rise.

Arrival as a Practice, Not a Point

Here is the shift.

Not a dramatic breakthrough, but a quiet recalibration. A subtle yet powerful reorientation—from chasing fulfillment to *choosing* it.

It begins when achievement stops being your identity and becomes your expression. You are no longer proving your worth with every milestone. You are simply revealing who you already are—through what you build, create, and contribute.

You stop saying, "I'll be happy when," and instead say, "I choose contentment now, even as I grow." You begin to understand that peace is not the reward for relentless striving—it is the foundation for meaningful progress. You are allowed to want more. But you no longer use that desire to delay your sense of *"enough-ness."*

And most importantly, you stop seeing arrival as a finish line. You start seeing it as a way of being. It is not some distant point where everything finally makes sense. It is a repeated decision to come home to yourself in the middle of the process.

This is the heart of the Fulfillment Curve:

Learning to live in the tension where striving and stillness can coexist. Where you can be fully engaged with your growth—without being owned by it. Where ambition no longer drowns out presence, but finds its rhythm within it.

To live this way is to realize that real momentum does not come from constant motion. It comes from aligned movement. From knowing where you are going, why it matters, and who you are becoming along the way.

Fulfillment is not a prize waiting at the top.

It is a posture.

A practice.

A quiet, repeated return to what matters most.

Reflection Prompt: Practicing Arrival

Fulfillment does not just arrive—it asks to be noticed.

To step off the treadmill of constant striving, we need more than insight. We need intention.

This is where the curve begins to bend. Not in a rush of clarity, but in a quiet moment of honesty. A pause. A breath. A willingness to look inward—not to judge, but to *see*.

These questions are not designed to produce immediate answers. They are meant to interrupt the trance of postponement. To help you listen—gently and truthfully—to what is real beneath the rush.

Ask yourself:

- What have I achieved that did not feel as good as I thought it would?

  Let yourself revisit that moment—not to diminish the effort, but to understand the expectation.

  Was the emptiness about the goal itself, or the hope that achievement would fix something deeper?

45

- *Where in my life am I waiting to be happy?*

  Be honest here. Is there a "when" you have been attaching your peace to? "When the house sells." "When I'm in shape." "When the business scales."

  Notice how many of those conditions are quietly running your life.

- *What would it look like to feel fulfilled today—not later?*

  Not when the work is done. Not when the boxes are checked. What would it mean to arrive now—in this version of your life?

  What small shift—mental, emotional, or behavioral—could bring you closer to contentment without changing a single external thing?

These are not questions to rush through.

They are thresholds.

And the courage to sit with them is itself a kind of arrival.

Closing Thought: The Gift of Stopping

The finish line is always moving.

Every time we reach it, it moves a little farther, just out of reach.

That is the nature of ambition without awareness—it is insatiable.

It keeps us striving, stretching, proving… but never quite arriving.

But what if you stepped off the track?

What if you stopped mid-stride—not in defeat, but in awakening?

And asked yourself:

What am I really **running toward?** And what have I been **running from?**

Because joy, presence, and peace—the very things we hope success will one day grant us—they are not waiting at the end.

They are *here*, now.

Quiet. Unassuming. Always available.

You do not have to chase them.

You do not have to earn them. You just have to stop running long enough to *receive* them.

This is the quiet miracle of fulfillment:

- It does not shout.
- It does not demand.
- It invites.

And the moment you stop long enough to listen—to breathe, to see, to *be*—you will realize you were never really chasing a finish line. You were chasing a feeling.

And that feeling?

It was never out there.

It is been inside you the whole time—

waiting for you to stop, and come home.

Understanding Fulfillment

FROM CHASING TO CHOOSING

We all begin with momentum.

Whether we realize it or not,
much of our early life is built
on momentum—absorbing the
definitions handed to us, chasing
the ideals we are told matter,
following the well-lit path of
praise, performance, and proof.

For a time, this feels like progress. And in many ways, it is. There is no shame in that pursuit. We strive because we want to matter. We want to belong. We want to get it "right."

But at some point—quietly, and often inconveniently—something shifts. The applause grows quieter. The calendar grows fuller. The thrill of arrival feels increasingly fleeting. And we begin to wonder:

- Is this really it?
- Is this what I was chasing?
- And why does it not feel more fulfilling?

Part II marks the hinge of this journey.

It is the point where success begins to lose its shine—not because it is meaningless, but because it is incomplete. Here, we begin the sacred work of redefining what we are actually after. Not the version of success we were handed, but the one that fits *us*. Not the growth that impresses the world, but the growth that brings us home to ourselves.

This is the turning point—from external validation to internal alignment. From inherited ambition to self-authored meaning.

In *Chapter 4*, we question the definition of success itself. Whose voice shaped it? Whose values sustain it? And what would it mean to stop performing for approval and start living from authenticity? We begin to understand that fulfillment does not come from climbing faster—but from climbing the right mountain.

In *Chapter 5*, we examine a different kind of arrival—the *Satisfaction Threshold*. That quiet, radical moment when we realize we do not need to keep striving to prove our worth. We explore the courage it takes to say "enough," not as resignation but as reclamation. We discover that contentment is not the end of ambition—it is the beginning of discernment.

And in *Chapter 6*, we make space for stillness—not as a pause from life, but as a reentry into it. We learn that clarity is not something we chase—it is something we *listen* for. And that often, the life we are seeking is not ahead of us in some future achievement—but beneath us, waiting to be noticed in the moment we finally slow down.

Together, these chapters invite a new kind of success. One measured not by speed or status, but by coherence. Integrity. Peace. This is not about opting out. It is about opting in—to a life that actually fits. That feels right. That reflects who you are when no one is watching.

Part II is where the shift begins.

From proving to belonging.

From more to meaning.

From chasing… to choosing.

CHAPTER FOUR

Success is not always
external—introduce the idea
of internal benchmarks.

Redefining Success

WHOSE DEFINITION ARE YOU LIVING BY?

*S*uccess is one of the
most overused—
and least questioned—
words in our culture.

Everyone wants it. Everyone
is chasing it. But few people
stop to ask: What does
it actually mean? And
more importantly: Whose
definition am I living by?

From the moment we are old enough to be praised for achievement, we start absorbing invisible scripts. Get the good grades. Win the award. Get into the right school. Land the right job. Buy the house. Drive the car. Look the part. We are handed a formula before we even know we have the right to question it.

Western culture equates success with individual striving—an inheritance from a society that long praised productivity as virtue and wealth as moral reward. Sociologist Max Weber traced this mindset back to the Protestant work ethic, where material prosperity became a sign of spiritual worth.

We inherit ideas of success from our families, schools, media, and culture. For some, it is wealth. For others, it is titles, status, a certain lifestyle. But if it is not defined by you, it may never satisfy you.

And yet, it is easy to confuse default settings for personal truth.

We rarely pause long enough to audit our ambitions. We are too busy climbing ladders that may not even be leaned against the right wall.

This is not to say external achievements are inherently empty. They can be deeply rewarding—when they are aligned with our values. But there is a profound difference between achieving for approval and achieving from authenticity.

Psychologists Edward Deci and Richard Ryan call this distinction intrinsic vs. extrinsic motivation. Their Self-Determination Theory shows that intrinsic goals—growth, relationships, contribution—are linked to greater well-being and long-term fulfillment. Extrinsic goals—wealth, fame, image—are more often associated with anxiety, burnout, and dissatisfaction, even when achieved.

The first creates pressure. The second creates peace.

True fulfillment begins when we stop asking What will they think of me? And start asking What do I think of the life I am building?

Most of us are conditioned to live with an invisible audience. We perform, often unconsciously, for the approval of parents, peers, bosses, or even strangers online. We shape our choices—careers, relationships, even the clothes we wear—through the lens of What will they think of me?

But here is the trap: that audience is fickle. Its applause is inconsistent. And its expectations are ever-changing.

When your life is built around managing perceptions, it becomes a performance. You are not living in your life—you are living next to it, watching how it looks from the outside.

That is why the question "What do I think of the life I am building?" is so powerful. It is a return to sovereignty. It shifts your compass from external noise to internal truth.

It is not about isolation or selfishness. It is about integrity—living in alignment with what you actually believe, value, and want to experience.

This is the essence of fulfillment. Not perfection. Not applause. But coherence. When your inner life and outer life begin to match.

The Cost of Borrowed Definitions

Living by someone else's definition of success can look impressive on the outside—but feel hollow on the inside. It is the executive who has everything but joy. The overachiever who cannot sleep because they are haunted by a question they do not know how to ask. The influencer who performs happiness but feels invisible in their own home.

We do not end up here because we are broken. We end up here because we have been trained to trade authenticity for acceptance.

Most of us were rewarded for conforming early. Gold stars, praise, promotions. We learned to read the room. Play the role. Stay inside the lines. But over time, those lines become walls. And what once earned us approval begins to cost us ourselves. (Queue Harry Chapin's "Flowers are Red")

These are not personal failures. They are signals—gentle (and sometimes not-so-gentle) nudges that we have strayed too far from our own voice.

They often show up as restlessness. Burnout. Numbness. A quiet ache that something is off—even when everything "should" feel right.

You can win the game and still hate how it feels to play it.

That is the cost of living by borrowed definitions.

Philosopher Byung-Chul Han describes this as the tyranny of self-optimization—a system that disguises exhaustion as empowerment. And Alain de Botton reminds us that success, if not defined by us, can become a quiet form of self-betrayal.

When you climb a ladder that is not yours, the view from the top can be disorienting. What once looked like a dream may now feel like a trap.

We cannot keep measuring success with someone else's ruler and expect to feel whole. Because someone else's definition was not designed for your life. It was not made for your values, your rhythm, your soul.

Wholeness comes when the life you are living belongs to you.

The Courage to Redefine

It takes courage to question the narrative.

To pause long enough to ask:

- Who authored this version of success I have been chasing?
- Do I still believe in it?
- Does it even reflect who I am today?

Reclaiming your definition of success means entering the unknown. And in a culture obsessed with clarity and optics, that kind of internal inquiry can feel threatening.

But here is the truth:

---

you cannot **design a fulfilling life** using someone else's blueprint.

It is easier—at least on the surface—to stay on the track you have always been on. To keep checking boxes. To keep performing the part. To keep telling yourself, "This is just what people do."

But beneath that ease is a quiet cost: the erosion of self-trust.

To redefine success is not to reject ambition. It is to elevate it. To tether it to truth, not performance. To let it be the outward expression of inner clarity.

It is not a step backward. It is a return—to the life that actually fits.

That kind of honesty can be terrifying—especially when your current life works by society's standards. When the house is beautiful. When the résumé is impressive. When your identity has been built on external wins.

But if the external wins do not match your internal truth, you will feel it. You already do.

You must summon the courage to press pause on the chase and ask:

- What actually matters to me?
- Where did my current goals come from?
- Am I living a story that is mine—or just playing a role I was handed?

This is more than reflection. It is rebellion. It is stepping outside the current to ask if the river leads where you want to go.

This is the beginning of agency. The moment when you stop outsourcing your worth. When you stop performing your life and start living it.

When success is self-defined, it stops being a finish line and becomes a foundation. It is not just about achievement. It is about alignment. About living a life that matches your values on the inside and your actions on the outside.

- It is not what looks good on paper.
- It is what feels right in your soul.

Redefining success does not mean abandoning ambition. It means elevating it—so that your ambition becomes a tool for fulfillment, not just a race for recognition.

This is not about shrinking your dreams. It is about finally dreaming in your own language.

The Danger of the Default Definition

When you adopt society's version of success without examining it, you end up building a life that looks great from the outside—but feels hollow inside.

You check the boxes. You hit the milestones. You do everything right. But somehow, it does not feel right.

You wonder why the satisfaction does not last. Why the celebration feels empty. Why, after all the striving, all the winning, all the proving—you still feel disconnected.

What is that *something* that is missing?

It is you.

Because when success is defined by someone else, your life becomes a performance. A projection. A shell.

And no matter how impressive that shell becomes, it cannot substitute for self-connection.

The danger of the default definition is that it is rarely questioned. It is deeply embedded in our systems—education, media, workplace culture, even in casual conversations.

From a young age, we are taught to pursue the version of success that looks good on paper.

Default success scripts run quietly in the background. They show up as assumptions you never stop to examine:

- More is always better.
- Visibility equals value.
- Busyness means you matter.

But default does not mean destined.

These scripts are borrowed—from institutions, industries, families, and influencers. They do not account for nuance. For soul. For season. And the longer you follow them without reflection, the more likely you are to wake up successful and unfulfilled.

We never pause to ask: Who decided this? Does it reflect what I actually want? Is this success—or just social conditioning dressed up as ambition?

Default success offers external validation, but not internal meaning. It rewards compliance, but not authenticity. It demands achievement, but often at the cost of aliveness.

You can build a life that wins applause—and still feel like a stranger inside it.

The tragedy is not just in living someone else's story. It is in becoming so good at it that you forget your own voice.

But here is the truth: default settings are meant to be adjusted. They are starting points, not finish lines. The real danger is not in being handed a definition—it is in never taking the time to rewrite it.

Success vs. Fulfillment: The Outer & Inner Game

Success is typically external. It is visible. Measurable.

Often admired.

You can show it to others. A promotion. A title. A house. A follower count. It is about what you do, what you have accomplished, what you have acquired.

The world recognizes it. Applauds it. Rewards it. And because of that, it becomes addictive. It feels like proof that we are "doing life right."

But there is a quiet truth that often gets buried underneath the trophies and to-do lists.

It is the truth we sense in still moments, when the noise dies down. The subtle discomfort that creeps in after the applause fades. The nagging question that success cannot quite answer:

Why does this **not feel better?**

Fulfillment is internal. It is emotional. Spiritual. Often invisible.

It is not about what you do—It is about *why* you do it. And how it feels to live with that choice.

Fulfillment lives in the pauses, not the performance. It is the peace you feel at the end of the day. The sense that your life makes sense—to you. Even when no one is watching. Even when no one understands.

- Success is an outcome. Fulfillment is a state of being.
- Success is visible. Fulfillment is felt.
- Success impresses. Fulfillment sustains.

The world will always offer more goals. More ladders. More trophies.

But those are outer markers. And outer markers only satisfy when they echo an inner truth.

Fulfillment is the quiet yes behind your actions. The feeling that your days reflect your values. That your energy is being used, not just spent.

You can have success without fulfillment. But it will always feel like a performance.

They are not enemies. They can, and often do, coexist. But they are not the same—and confusing the two is where the trouble begins.

Because when you chase success without anchoring it in fulfillment, you can end up with a life that looks complete but feels empty.

THE
FULFILLMENT
curve

That is when burnout creeps in. When you hit the goal and wonder why it did not change anything. When confusion sets in, and you start to question whether you were climbing the right mountain at all. And eventually, if left unchecked, it can lead to regret—the realization that you were living by a script that was never yours.

- Success can impress. But fulfillment sustains.
- Success fills the calendar. Fulfillment fills the soul.

If you are only chasing success, you will always need more of it to feel okay. But if you are building your life on fulfillment, success becomes a byproduct—not the point.

The Pain of Misaligned Success

One of the most painful realizations is this:

- You can succeed at something that was never meant for you.
- You can do everything right. Follow the map. Hit the milestones. Collect the accolades. And still feel completely out of place in your own life.
- You can spend years climbing a ladder… Only to find it is been leaning against the wrong wall all along.

That is not just disappointing—it is disorienting. Because the world may be celebrating your arrival, while your soul is quietly mourning everything you abandoned to get there.

This happens when we override our own voice in favor of the voices around us. It happens when we let fear or obligation dictate our direction. When we build a life based on expectation instead of intention.

At first, it can look like momentum. You are making progress, you are advancing, you are getting noticed.

But if that momentum is not aligned with your values, your desires, your truth—then every step forward can feel like a step away from yourself.

You start to feel a subtle ache. Not because you have failed—but because you have succeeded in betraying your own needs.

This is the paradox of misaligned success:

- It looks like winning from the outside.
- But it feels like losing on the inside.

You may not even notice it at first. You are busy. You are productive. You are admired. But under the surface, there is a quiet erosion—of joy, of clarity, of peace.

Eventually, that erosion becomes undeniable.

You can hit the mark and still feel empty. Not because you did not try hard enough—but because the target was never yours.

That is when the truth breaks through: You have been living a version of success that does not fit your life—and never really did.

This is one of the hardest truths to face: that you might be celebrated for living a life that does not actually honor who you are.

It is not failure. It is misalignment.

And when you realize that misalignment, you have a choice:

Double down on the image.

Or come home to the truth.

It is Time To Take The Pen Back

At some point, you have to stop living the story you inherited—and start writing the one that is yours.

To stop letting the world dictate what your life should look like. To reclaim authorship over your choices, your values, your definition of enough. To stop chasing someone else's version of success—and begin creating your own vision of fulfillment.

This is not an easy step. It requires unlearning. Shedding. Pausing long enough to listen for a voice that has been drowned out for years—your own.

But this is where true change begins: Not with doing more. But with choosing better.

To define success on your terms, you have to start asking different questions.

- Not, *How do I get ahead?*
- But, *Where am I actually trying to go—and why?*
- Not, *What will they think of me?*
- But, *What do I think of the life I am living?*

Here are some new questions to ask yourself—Questions that do not just measure achievement, but illuminate alignment:

- **What does a rich life look like for me—emotionally, mentally, spiritually, relationally?**
  What kind of inner world do I want to cultivate?
  How do I want to feel when I wake up in the morning?
- **What are the values I want my life to reflect?**
  Not the ones I inherited. Not the ones I am expected to have. But the ones that feel true—even if they go against the grain.
- **What does enough look like—and how will I know when I have reached it?**
  How do I define sufficiency—not in terms of scarcity, but in terms of peace? What would it mean to be content, not complacent?

These are not soft questions. They are radical. Because they return authorship to where it belongs: you.

The answers may surprise you. They may be quieter than you expect. They may challenge the life you have built. They may require you to let go of long-held ambitions or identities you have worn like armor.

But they will set you free.

You do not have to keep living a script you did not write.

Because when your life is aligned with what you value, you no longer have to chase fulfillment—you live it.

Not as a destination, but as a daily practice. Not as a prize to be won, but as a path to be walked.

This is the beginning of a new kind of success. The kind that does not just impress others—but deeply fulfills you.

Living Your Definition

When you begin to live your own definition of success, everything changes.

- You set fewer goals—but they are deeper.
- You say yes more intentionally. No more easily.
- You stop comparing your pace to someone else's.
- You protect what restores you.

This is what it means to live aligned:

- To define, not perform.
- To express, not impress.
- To build a life that fits from the inside out.

Once you have redefined success on your own terms, something subtle but profound begins to shift.

THE
FULFILLMENT
curve

You stop living by default. You stop measuring your life with someone else's metrics. And you start making choices that actually feel right—even if they do not look flashy from the outside.

You will start living differently:

- **You will pursue fewer things—but with greater depth.**
  No longer scattered across a dozen obligations that do not move the needle for you. You will go deeper into what matters, rather than wider into what does not.

- **You will say no more easily, and yes more intentionally.**
  Your time and energy will become sacred. You will not need to prove yourself through overcommitting or overperforming. Your boundaries will reflect your clarity—not your guilt.

- **You will stop comparing your life to someone else's highlight reel.**
  Because you will know what you are building. You will trust your own timing. You will not need the noise of external validation when you have the signal of internal alignment.

This does not mean your life becomes effortless. It means you become energized. You will still work hard—but it will be work that aligns with your values. You will still face challenges—but they will feel like growth, not grind.

Your path will still involve effort—but it will be fueled by meaning, not pressure.

And that makes all the difference.

You will begin to notice something else, too: a kind of quiet joy. Not the high of achievement, but the steadiness of peace. Not the thrill of approval, but the richness of self-respect.

Because when you define success on your terms, you no longer need to chase your life. ***You get to inhabit it.***

Fully. Freely. And finally—fulfilled.

Reflection Prompts

But awareness alone is not enough. Insight must lead to inquiry. Redefining success is not just a decision—it is a practice. And that practice begins by getting honest with yourself.

You cannot build a meaningful life if you do not first uncover the foundation you have been standing on. You have to trace the roots of your definition. Ask where it came from. Ask whether it is still serving you—or if it ever did.

This is where the real work begins. Not in adding more to your plate, but in peeling back the layers.

To move forward with clarity, you must pause long enough to ask the questions that rarely get asked.

- What definition of success have I been living by?
- Where did it come from?
- If I could rewrite my success story today, what would change?

Take your time. Be honest. There are no wrong answers—only revealing ones.

This is your moment to take the pen back. To stop performing and start creating. To begin not just a new chapter—but your true one.

Closing Thought

Success without fulfillment is achievement without peace. It is reaching the top of the mountain—only to realize it is not the view you wanted. It is winning the game but feeling no joy in the victory. It is the applause fading faster than the emptiness that follows.

We have been taught to chase milestones. To accumulate, to impress, to conquer. But fulfillment asks a different question: **Is the life I am building true to who I am?**

When you redefine success around what truly matters to you, everything shifts. Your goals become rooted in meaning. Your pace becomes sustainable. Your choices become clearer—not because life gets easier, but because you get more honest.

You stop striving to prove your worth. And start creating a life that reflects it.

This is not the end of ambition. It is the beginning of alignment.

Because in the end, a rich life is not measured by how much you have achieved—but by how deeply you have lived.

Do not just chase milestones.

Build a life.

Your life.

5

How to recognize when you
have "arrived" and why it is
okay to feel complete.

The Satisfaction Threshold

THE MYTH OF LIMITLESS GROWTH

*I*n business, we hear it all the time:
"If you are not growing,
you are dying."

It is become more than a strategy—it
is become a belief system. One
we have adopted not only for
companies, but for ourselves.

It is a seductive mantra. Growth
equals life, we are told. Expansion
is success. Stasis is failure.

But what happens when this belief system slips past the boardroom and into our bloodstream?

We have absorbed the idea that more is always better. More money. More reach. More followers. More recognition. More goals. More output. More proof that we are still relevant, still rising, still in motion.

And just like that, "growth" becomes our default setting. Not strategic. Not intentional. Just expected.

In economics, limitless growth is unsustainable. In human life, it is exhausting. But somewhere along the way, we internalized the belief that unless we are expanding, we are failing.

This is the myth of limitless growth—that happiness, satisfaction, and self-worth are always just beyond the next milestone. That arrival is a mirage we must keep chasing.

But here is the quiet truth: In the pursuit of "more," we often lose sight of "enough." And enough is the birthplace of fulfillment.

The Trouble with More

Growth, in its proper place, is not the enemy. It is natural, even necessary at times. But when growth becomes compulsive, we stop growing and start grasping.

We become addicted to accumulation—not just of things, but of identity. The title. The income bracket. The achievement. The admiration.

We do not pause to ask if these things are actually satisfying. We just assume they should be.

This is the paradox: the more we achieve, the harder it becomes to tell whether we are climbing a meaningful mountain—or just scaling a ladder with no top.

We keep going because we can. And because we are afraid to stop.

What Is the Satisfaction Threshold?

We spend much of our lives chasing an abstract summit—believing that if we just achieve a little more, earn a little more, improve a little more, we will finally feel whole.

But what if the sense of arrival we seek is not found in more, but in alignment?

The Satisfaction Threshold is the point at which your internal sense of peace meets your external reality. It is the intersection where what you have matches what you need—not just materially, but emotionally and spiritually.

It is not marked by applause or headlines. It is not something others will always understand. It is a quiet place. A felt sense. A moment where you exhale and think:

- This is working.
- This is whole.
- I am okay here.

And that moment is everything.

It is not the absence of desire—but the presence of perspective. It is where striving pauses long enough to let gratitude catch up.

It is the place where you feel grounded. Grateful. Complete. Not because everything is perfect—but because you recognize what you have is already enough.

We have been taught to equate satisfaction with stagnation. To rest is to risk falling behind. To say "enough" is to appear unambitious.

But the truth is: satisfaction is not complacency. It is not laziness. It is clarity.

And in a world obsessed with expansion, **clarity is power.**

At the Satisfaction Threshold, growth becomes optional, not obligatory. It is no longer the thing you chase for validation—but the thing you choose from alignment.

It is here you gain the freedom to ask better questions:

- What brings peace, not just pride?
- What deepens my days, not just fills them?
- What serves my soul—not just my status?

And suddenly, the game changes.

Because when you stop needing everything to be more—you begin to notice what is already meaningful.

This threshold is not always visible from the outside. There is no neon sign. No victory parade. No one clapping at the finish line.

But you will know when you have crossed it.

Because chasing no longer feels like living.

It will feel like noise.

And in that silence, something new arises: Presence. Purpose. A quiet, rooted sense that this life you are living—It is already rich.

Signs You Have Reached the Satisfaction Threshold

You may not see it on a spreadsheet. But you will feel it in your body.

Here are subtle signals that you have arrived—whether you knew it or not.

You feel at peace without needing to explain why.

You stop justifying your choices. You no longer need external validation to feel aligned.

You feel a deep "yes" to what you have built.

Your work, your life, your relationships—however imperfect— feel rooted in something true.

You no longer measure success by comparison.

Other people's progress does not rattle you. Their "more" does not make you feel like "less."

You can say "no" without guilt.

Ambition is still there—but it is quieter now. You choose what matters, and release what does not.

You crave presence more than progress.

You are drawn to stillness. Simplicity feels like wealth. You would rather enjoy than optimize.

You experience joy in the ordinary.

Small pleasures—sunlight, silence, a conversation—feel full. You stop waiting for the next big thing.

The Satisfaction Threshold is not a finish line. It is a frequency. When you are in it, you know. And when you drift, you can return.

The Dopamine Rollercoaster

We are neurologically wired to pursue more. Every achievement delivers a hit of dopamine—a biochemical reward that motivates us to keep going. But our brains adapt quickly. Today's high becomes tomorrow's baseline. That sense of satisfaction fades, and we start chasing the next win.

Psychologists call this hedonic adaptation—a treadmill where today's thrill becomes tomorrow's normal. And when the high fades, we raise the stakes again, hoping to reclaim the feeling. But that feeling cannot be chased forever.

That is why even big accomplishments can feel strangely fleeting. Not because they did not matter, but because our inner experience quickly recalibrates. The applause fades. The inbox refills. The climb continues.

And if we do not pause long enough to notice the pattern, we end up mistaking stimulation for satisfaction. Momentum for meaning. Dopamine for depth.

Why We Struggle to Know When We Have Arrived

If the Satisfaction Threshold is the place where peace and purpose meet— why is it so hard to find?

Most of us do not know where our threshold is for one simple reason: We never paused to define it.

We created goals but not limits. We celebrated the stretch but ignored the stillness. We attached our worth to progress, and made peace feel like stagnation.

We were taught how to set goals, but not how to recognize completion. We were trained to stretch, but not to stay. To optimize, but not to observe. We learned to equate movement with meaning—and in doing so, we made stillness feel like failure.

Even when we do arrive somewhere meaningful, we often miss it. Why? Because our eyes are already fixed on the next horizon. Instead of inhabiting the moment, we scan past it—conditioned to believe there is always something better just out of frame.

And beneath that constant scanning is **fear.**

The fear that if we stop, we will fall behind. That someone else will pass us. That the momentum we have built will vanish—and take our worth with it.

We fear irrelevance. Or laziness. Or worse: that without striving, we will not know who we are.

Worse yet, we fear what might rise in the silence: Questions we have avoided. Truths we have delayed. An identity built so entirely on doing that we no longer know how to simply be.

So we keep going. Adding. Pushing. Upgrading. Until life becomes an endless series of sprints with no finish line—just the illusion of one.

But here is the paradox: The more we add, the more elusive satisfaction becomes.

Because fulfillment is not found in accumulation. It is found in alignment.

Satisfaction Is Not the Same as Settling

This is where many of us get stuck.

We finally begin to feel a sense of peace—only to doubt it. We hesitate. Second-guess. Because we have been conditioned to confuse satisfaction with settling.

So, let's be clear about something essential: Satisfaction is not giving up on your potential. It is not waving a white flag or stepping off the playing field. It is not shrinking your dreams to fit someone else's definition of "realistic."

In fact, it may be the bravest move you make.

Because true satisfaction does not arise from passivity—**it comes from discernment.**

Discernment is what allows you to pause in a moment of momentum and ask the deeper questions:

- Is this growth aligned with who I am becoming?
- Or is it driven by fear of being forgotten, overlooked, or outpaced?

It is the difference between pushing forward and being pulled forward—between ego-driven striving and soul-driven direction.

Satisfaction, then, is not the absence of ambition. It is the presence of alignment.

Psychologists studying sufficiency and minimalism have found that the feeling of "enough"—not more—is strongly correlated with peace, gratitude, and well-being. Enough is not settling. It is sovereignty.

Journaling Prompt: Mastery Over Momentum

Here is a journaling prompt to follow the section on Satisfaction Is Not the Same as Settling, designed to help readers explore their own relationship with ambition, alignment, and the fear of "settling".

Take a quiet moment and reflect on the following:

Where in my life am I still pushing forward—not because I truly want to, but because I feel I should?

What is motivating that drive?
Is it fear? Ego? A need to prove something?

Now consider:

What would it look like to pause—not out of weakness, but out of wisdom?

What would I let go of if I trusted that I am already enough?
What does aligned growth feel like compared to forced progress?

Finally:

Where in my life am I being called not to climb higher, but to go deeper?

What might I discover if I stopped trying to "get ahead"
and started honoring where I already am?

It is knowing when your ambition is in service of your essence—and when it is being hijacked by fear, ego, or comparison.

It is the clarity to ask not just can I go further, but should I?

Will this next level actually expand my life—or will it just clutter it? Will it offer depth—or just distraction?

This is where many achievers face their greatest reckoning. Because the world will always cheer your progress, even when that progress is pulling you away from yourself.

That is why this kind of discernment matters.

In it lies what I call *mastery over momentum*: The ability to move from intention, not inertia. To choose your next step not because the world demands it, but because you do.

And in that choice, you reclaim the richest form of power: Not the power to do more, but the wisdom to do right.

The Shift from Striving to Savoring

To live at the Satisfaction Threshold is to shift from striving to savoring.

It is not the end of ambition— but the **redefinition of it.**

Ambition becomes a tool, not a tether. It serves your values, not your ego. It supports your life—it does not become your life.

You still grow. But now, you grow from choice, not compulsion. You still dream. But your dreams are aligned with who you are, not who you are trying to impress.

Contentment does not mean passivity. It means presence. It is a form of wholeness rooted not in arrival, but in acceptance. It says:

This moment counts, even if nothing changes.

The Art of Declaring 'Enough'

There is a quiet strength in saying:

- "This is good."
- "This is working."
- "I don't need to chase something just because I can."

That kind of pause is not weakness. It is wisdom. It is the moment you stop running long enough to realize… you have already arrived somewhere beautiful.

Psychological and spiritual traditions across cultures affirm this idea. From Buddhist non-attachment to Stoic tranquility, from minimalist living to sufficiency mindset—the essence is the same: fulfillment comes not from accumulation, but from alignment.

Psychologists studying contentment confirm that it is distinct from pleasure or happiness. It is grounded in clarity, emotional balance, and freedom from craving. It is not static—it is intentional.

It is the whisper that says: You do not need more to matter. You just need to live what matters most.

In a world addicted to acceleration, knowing when to stop is a revolutionary act.

The Rhythm of Expansion and Rest

Fulfillment lives in rhythm.

There are seasons to grow—and seasons to dwell. Moments to stretch—and moments to savor.

The Satisfaction Threshold is not a line you cross once. It is a feeling you learn to honor, again and again. It asks:

- What season am I in now?
- What would enough look like here?

Because fulfillment does not come from always doing more. It comes from knowing when what you have—and who you are—is enough.

And once you know that, growth becomes a choice, not a compulsion.

Fulfillment Is Found in Enough

In a world shouting "more," there is something radical about whispering "enough." It is not resignation. It is sovereignty.

Enough is not the end of growth.
It is the beginning of discernment.

Because when you know what is enough for *you*—not for your peers, your parents, or your projections—you stop needing to measure your worth by someone else's yardstick. You begin to understand that real fulfillment does not come from the next upgrade or milestone. It comes from being deeply rooted in the present, aware of what already surrounds you, and clear on what truly matters.

This clarity quiets the noise. You start to recognize richness in stillness. You begin to feel the texture of your life again—not as something to fix, but something to feel. And in that stillness, you might notice something surprising: you already have much of what you once believed was missing.

And that, perhaps, is the beginning of true wealth.

Questions to Find Your Satisfaction Threshold

- What am I pursuing that no longer brings joy or meaning?
- What would enough look like for me—
  financially, emotionally, spiritually?
- If I never achieved more than this, could I still feel whole?

Reflection Prompts

Striving can feel noble. Productive. Even virtuous. But sometimes it is just a habit—one that keeps us always reaching, never resting.

We get so used to the climb, we forget to notice when we've already arrived. When the life we once longed for is quietly unfolding... but we are too busy to feel it.

What if fulfillment is not something you earn—but something you allow?

Take a breath. Look again. Let these questions guide you toward the grace of enough.

- In what areas of my life am I always striving?
- Where might I already be "there," but
  have not allowed myself to feel it?
- How would my life feel if I trusted that I already had enough?

You do not have to abandon growth. Just remember to let it land. The goal is not more. It's meaning.

Closing Thought

We live in a culture that glorifies growth and movement. But not all forward motion leads to fulfillment.

The deeper work is not in the chase—but in the choice. The choice to pause. To feel. To declare, even for a moment:

"This is **enough.**"

And that simple truth? That is where the real wealth lives.

Fulfillment begins not with reaching more—but with recognizing enough.

The Satisfaction Threshold is not a retreat from growth. It is the foundation for wiser, more grounded expansion.

Because when you no longer chase from lack, you begin to build from peace. And that is where the richest kind of growth begins.

6

CHAPTER SIX

In a world of
doing, we need
time for being.

The Role of Stillness

We are taught to run. In a world of instant messages, real-time updates, and 24/7 productivity hacks, stillness feels almost rebellious. It is uncomfortable. It is unfamiliar. It is quiet.

But in that quiet lives everything we say we want: Clarity. Direction. Peace. Presence.

Stillness is not a break from life. It is life, unmasked.

THE
FULFILLMENT
curve

And yet, we resist it. We fill the silence with plans, notifications, next steps—afraid that if we ever truly stop, we will lose our edge, our identity, our place in the race.

But what if the race itself **was the illusion?**

What if everything we have been chasing—purpose, clarity, meaning—has been waiting, quietly, beneath the noise?

Stillness does not just reveal life. It reveals us. Who we are without the striving. What we value without the pressure. Where we belong when we are no longer proving.

It is in this pause—not dramatic, but deliberate—that a new kind of momentum begins. Not the momentum of acceleration, but of alignment.

Why We Resist Stillness

Stillness can be terrifying—because in stillness, there are no distractions. No metrics to check. No applause to chase. Just us. Ourselves. Our inner voice.

And sometimes, we do not like what we hear. So, we fill the silence with busyness. We confuse activity with purpose.

But here is the truth: Fulfillment does not yell. It whispers. And if your life is too loud, you will miss it.

We do not often admit it, but silence can feel like a confrontation. Not with the world—but with ourselves. Because in that quiet, we are left with the unedited version of our lives. The doubts we have muted.

The grief we have shelved. The questions we have buried beneath productivity and performance.

Stillness does not create discomfort—it reveals it. And that revelation is where the real work begins.

It is easier to chase a new goal than to sit with an unmet need. Easier to check another box than to ask if the boxes even matter.

But if we are willing to listen—really listen—that whisper can guide us somewhere deeper than success ever could.

The Stoics called this tranquility—the strength to be unmoved by noise. Buddhists teach that non-reactivity is not apathy, but awareness. Stillness is not avoidance. It is the willingness to meet life as it is, without flinching.

Toward a life that is not just full... But fulfilling.

Stillness Is Where *Alignment* Happens

In stillness, we reconnect with:

- Our values (what really matters)
- Our energy (what is draining or renewing us)
- Our truth (what we have been avoiding)

Stillness is not about doing nothing. It is about doing less—so we can hear more.

It is the space between stimulus and response. The breath before the next decision. It is where we ask the question, "Is this the life I want?"—and actually wait for the answer.

Most of us move too fast to notice when we have veered off course. We chase goals out of habit. Say yes out of guilt. Follow routines we

curve

never meant to build. And slowly, quietly, we *drift*—from our purpose, our peace, ourselves.

Stillness is how we find our way back. Not by force or strategy—but by listening.

Neuroscience confirms this, too. During quiet reflection, our brains activate what researchers call the default mode network—a space where insight, memory, and meaning converge. It is not empty time. It is deep mental processing—the soil where clarity takes root.

Mindfulness research shows that intentional pauses improve decision-making, helping us act from clarity instead of compulsion. Stillness does not slow us down—it sharpens how we move forward.

It is in the pause that we begin to recognize what feels true. Where tension lives in the body. Where resentment lingers beneath routine. Where desire stirs beneath duty.

This is where alignment begins—not as a dramatic shift, but as a gentle re-centering. A quiet recalibration of how we spend our time, our attention, our lives.

Alignment is when the inner and outer self begin to speak the same language.

Like adjusting the lens on a camera, stillness sharpens the image. What was once a blur of obligations becomes a picture of what actually matters.

Because fulfillment does not come from doing more. It comes from doing what matters—on purpose.

Forms of Stillness

Stillness does not require a meditation cushion or a perfect setting. It does not always look the way we expect. More often, it shows up in the spaces we overlook—the pause before a reply, the walk we take without our phone, the moment we choose to journal instead of scroll.

It might be a morning without an agenda. No checklist. No rush. Just enough openness to notice how you feel before the world asks for anything. It might be a few deep breaths before a meeting. A reset, not a ritual.

Stillness is not the absence of movement. It is the presence of attention. Not doing nothing—but doing *this*, with full awareness.

These moments do not shout. But they signal something important: a *shift* in how we relate to time, attention, and ourselves. What first feels like inefficiency becomes something else entirely—a return to rhythm. A quiet re-centering.

Stillness creates just enough space for clarity to surface. Not through force, but through awareness. We stop rushing. We start listening. And slowly, we begin to act from intention rather than inertia.

Because when we protect small pockets of stillness, we begin to feel the difference between reacting and responding. Between distraction and direction. Between living fast—and living aligned.

Stillness is not withdrawal. It is not escape. It is reentry. Back into your own rhythm. Back into clarity. Back into yourself.

This is where fulfillment begins—not in the future, but in the pause that lets us hear what we have been missing.

Stillness in Practice

1. Stillness as Self-Permission

Stillness is not always convenient. In a culture that rewards urgency, carving out moments of stillness can feel selfish—or even lazy. But that is often the first barrier to overcome: the belief that stillness must be earned or justified.

In truth, stillness is not a reward for getting everything done. It is the foundation that helps us decide what is worth doing in the first place.

2. Stillness in Motion

Stillness does not mean stopping. It means slowing your inner pace, even while life moves around you. You can experience stillness on a bike ride, in a long drive without music, or while doing the dishes with your full attention.

It is not about escape. It is about presence.

And presence can happen anywhere—even in motion—when your mind stops racing ahead or spinning behind.

3. The Discomfort of Stillness

Not all stillness feels peaceful. Sometimes, when the noise fades, we are left with things we have avoided: grief, regret, confusion. That is part of the work.

Stillness does not always soothe—it reveals. And it is in those revelations that we begin to understand what is truly misaligned.

4. Stillness as a Daily Rhythm

Stillness is not one big moment. It is a practice. A rhythm. Something you return to like breath—again and again.

The more familiar it becomes, the more accessible it feels. And over time, it shifts how you move through the rest of your life.

How Do We Drift?

Drift is rarely dramatic. It does not come with alarms. It happens slowly—quietly—under the surface of a busy life.

You take on more. You stop asking why. You move from one thing to the next without checking whether it still fits.

At first, it looks like adaptability. Responsibility. Even success.

But over time, something shifts. You feel disconnected from your own calendar. Your days get filled but not fulfilled. You start to notice a gap between what you are doing and what you care about—between how you spend your time and what actually brings you alive.

That gap is drift.

It shows up in the small compromises. The quick yes. The skipped walk. The moments when you override your intuition to meet someone else's urgency. It is subtle. Often well-intentioned. But over time, it adds up.

We do not drift because we are careless. We drift because we stop paying attention. We stop listening to the part of us that knows what matters—and start responding to everything else.

Drift is the space between living reactively and living on purpose.

The good news is, once you name it, you can start to notice it. And once you notice it, you can come back.

Not with a massive life overhaul. But with one clear choice at a time.

A pause. A no. A redirect. A return.

That is the beginning of realignment.

THE
FULLFILLMENT
curve

Stillness Is Not Laziness

Our culture equates rest with weakness. We have been conditioned to believe that productivity is the same as worth—and that
slowing down means falling behind. But stillness is not laziness. It
is a discipline.

It takes strength to pause. Strength to resist the pressure to prove.
Strength to say, *"I will not be owned by urgency."*

Stillness asks us to trust something deeper than momentum. To
believe that our value does not come from how much we produce,
and that nothing meaningful will collapse if we take a moment to
be, instead of always doing.

This runs counter to everything we have been taught. Hustle is
rewarded. Speed is praised. Noise is mistaken for importance. So,
when we choose stillness, we are not stepping out of life—we are
stepping into it more fully. With intention. With clarity. With control
over where our energy goes.

Stillness is not the absence of ambition. It is the refinement of it.
It is the shift from reacting to everything to creating something that
actually matters.

That is not weakness. That is wisdom.

And it is where fulfillment begins—not as the reward for slowing
down, but as the natural result of coming back to what matters.

What Stillness Reveals

Stillness is not just a pause. It is a mirror. A lens. A quiet space
where the noise settles—and what is underneath begins to show.

When you stop moving long enough to listen, you start to notice what has been driving you. Sometimes, that movement is fueled by clarity. But sometimes, it is coping in disguise.

Stillness reveals if *chasing* has become your way of avoiding—avoiding discomfort, avoiding silence, avoiding the deeper questions that do not have quick answers. It reveals whether your goals are truly yours, or simply what you thought you were supposed to want.

It shows you if your life reflects your values—or your fears. If your schedule is a reflection of what matters, or a reaction to what others expect. If you are living with intention, or simply inhabiting a story someone else handed you.

Stillness does not judge. It does not demand. It just makes things visible. It sharpens the image. Stillness is the lens that brings your life into focus.

And in that clarity, you can finally ask:

- Is this aligned?
- Is this sustainable?
- Is this *mine*?

Because you cannot recalibrate what you cannot see. And you cannot live fulfilled if you are not willing to look.

Stillness is the lens that brings your life into focus.

Returning to Stillness: The 10-Minute Check-In

Here is a simple way to begin. Nothing complex. No device. No music. No plan.

Just sit. Let your breath slow. Let the noise settle.

Then ask yourself: *What is alive in me right now?*

Do not rush the answer. Do not try to fix it. Just listen. Feel what is there—without judgment, without agenda.

When something rises—a thought, a feeling, a tension, a truth—write it down. One insight. One honest line. Carry it into your day like a compass, not a command.

The more often you return to stillness, the more familiar it becomes. Not as escape, but as anchor. A place you can return to. A place that reminds you who you are, and what matters now.

Story Vignette:
The Drive That Changed Nothing (and Everything)

It was a Tuesday afternoon. Nothing remarkable about it—except that I had forty minutes between meetings and nowhere I *had* to be. Normally, I would fill the gap. Check emails. Return a call. Do something to prove I was using my time well.

But that day, I did not. I got in the car and started driving with no destination. I did not turn on a podcast. I did not check the clock. I just drove.

At first, my mind did what it always does—it filled the space. Old conversations. To-do lists. A few arguments I should have won. But eventually, even that noise began to thin. I noticed the light slanting across the windshield. The sound of the tires on the road. The way my breath had settled.

There was no epiphany. No breakthrough. Just a surprising sense of steadiness. I had not realized how tense I had been until I was not.

I did not accomplish anything on that drive. But when I walked into my next meeting, I was different. Quieter, but clearer. More available—less reactive. And it struck me how rare that feeling was. Not from doing more. But from finally doing less.

I would not have called it stillness then. But now I know—that is exactly what it was.

Reflection Prompt:

Where in your daily life do you tend to fill space out of habit—rather than need?

Think about the first 10 minutes of your morning. The time between meetings. The moment you reach for your phone in line at the store. What would it feel like to leave even one of those spaces open?

Not for productivity. Not for optimization.

But simply to listen—for what is true, what is stirring, what is waiting to be noticed.

Try it. Just once.

Then ask yourself:

- What did I notice that I usually miss?
- What am I afraid I will feel if I slow down?
- When do I feel most present and grounded?
- How can I create more stillness in my daily life?

Closing Thought

Stillness is not the opposite of achievement. It is the soil in which it grows.

We are taught that progress comes from movement—more effort, more action, more doing. But real progress begins with awareness. With the courage to pause. With the clarity to ask:

Is this the **right direction?**

Stillness gives you that clarity. It helps you see what is essential before you spend energy pursuing what is not.

It does not pull you away from achievement. It brings you closer to the kind that actually fulfills you.

Because when you make space to listen—truly listen—you no longer chase meaning. You begin to live it.

Not in some distant, ideal future. But here. Now. In the life you are already in.

In the choices you begin to make—on purpose.

Through the Curve

A PERSONAL REFLECTION

In 1989, I returned to
the family business with
a chip on my shoulder.
I was young, intense,
and carrying the weight
of something to prove.
Fulfillment was not even
in my vocabulary—I
was fueled by drive. By
ambition. By the kind of
hunger that does not pause
to ask deeper questions.

Balance? I was aware
of it. I respected it. But it
did not shape my decisions.

And while I never worshipped
the cult of more, I certainly believed
in the power of momentum.

I was moving fast, climbing
quickly, learning constantly.

I was growing.

But somewhere along the way, a quiet
mismatch began to emerge.

Professionally, things looked good. Personally,
something was missing. I did not know it at
the time, but I had begun climbing a ladder
that was leaning against the wrong wall.

And then—everything fell apart.

What followed was a furnace. A
stripping down. A season where
everything I had used to define
myself was tested—or taken.

I questioned everything I
believed. I wrestled in the
dark. There were moments that
did not feel real. Moments that
bent time and belief. Almost like a
waking dream—or an hallucination. The
kind of moments that leave you changed
forever, even if you cannot explain why.

I came out the other side—clearer, in some
ways. More rooted. But tired. Worn. Changed.

And now, decades later, as I build again—this time,
multiple brands, a broader vision, a more integrated
life—I find myself driven by something different.

Not achievement.
Not approval.
Fulfillment.

It is no longer an afterthought. It is
the filter. The compass. The fuel.

That season taught me what
matters—and what does not.

And it is why I wrote this book.

III

Elevate and Ground

WHERE FULFILLMENT BECOMES PRACTICE

Redefining success is a powerful beginning.

Recognizing your Satisfaction Threshold
is a vital shift. Returning to stillness gives
you the clarity to see what truly matters.

But insight alone is not enough.

Eventually, every internal breakthrough
asks the same question:

Now what?

That is where this part of the journey begins. Not with more theory, but with a return to practice. A return to the rhythms, rituals, and structures that help you live your truth—not just realize it.

Because fulfillment is not a one-time revelation. It is a way of building. A way of choosing. A way of showing up—daily, imperfectly, and intentionally—in a life that both lifts you and holds you steady.

Part 3 is where the abstract becomes embodied.

Where you move beyond clarity into creation.

Where you begin designing a life that does not just look good—but *feels* right.

Not in fleeting moments, but in the daily architecture of how you work, rest, relate, and grow.

In *Chapter 7*, we explore goal-setting through a new lens—not as a performance to perfect, but as a reflection of your soul. You will learn how to translate inner alignment into external action, setting goals that energize, not exhaust. That express your values, not your fear. That move you forward without pulling you apart.

In *Chapter 8*, we let go of the glorified grind. We reimagine growth not as a frantic climb, but as a rhythmic unfolding. You will discover what sustainable, soul-rooted expansion looks like—and how to grow in ways that nourish rather than deplete. This is growth that breathes. That listens. That lasts.

And in *Chapter 9*, we give fulfillment structure. Through the Fulfillment Framework—a living system of filters, audits, and reflection tools—you will gain the clarity and rhythm needed to stay aligned in a world that constantly pulls you off course. This is not another productivity hack. It is a compass for building the life that actually fits you.

This part is where fulfillment becomes design.

Where your days begin to reflect your decisions.

Where success is no longer something you chase—but something you *inhabit*.

To elevate is to rise into possibility.

To be grounded is to remain connected to what matters. You need both.

This is where you learn to build a life that gives you both. Let's begin.

7

How to make achievement
serve fulfillment—not the
other way around.

Beyond the Checklist

*W*e are taught,
almost from the beginning,
that life is a race.

Pick your lane. Get ahead.
Stay busy. Measure up.

And somewhere along the way,
without even realizing it, we begin
to link our value to our velocity.
We learn to define a "good year"
by how much we accomplished.
A "successful life" by how much
we achieved. A "worthy self"
by how well we kept pace.

But underneath the productivity… beneath the metrics and the milestones… there is a quieter question that rarely gets asked:

What is all this for?

Not in a cynical way. But in an honest, curious, soul-searching way.

Because for all the talk about vision boards, KPIs, and five-year plans, what most of us are really searching for is not more output. It is more meaning.

- We want our goals to matter.
- We want our efforts to reflect something true.
- We want to grow, yes—but in the direction of wholeness, not just performance.

This chapter is an invitation to pause and reconsider what it means to "set a goal."

Not as a box to check. But as a path back to yourself.

This is the quiet question beneath the hustle.

Setting Goals that Reflect Your Soul

What if your goals are not broken—but the reasons you set them are?

We live in a culture that worships the checklist. We track, optimize, gamify—believing that if we just do more, climb higher, or hustle harder, something meaningful will finally click into place.

And sometimes, it does.

Goals can be thrilling. They give us momentum, clarity, even hope. They can lift us from stagnation, sharpen our focus, and challenge our limits.

But, have you ever crossed a finish line only to feel… nothing? Or, have you ever worked relentlessly toward a goal, only to wonder why you are not any closer to peace or joy?

Then you already know:

It is not the goal that is the problem.
It is what is driving it.

Psychologists studying motivation have found that goals rooted in personal values—like connection, growth, or contribution—lead to greater resilience and long-term well-being. But when goals are based on image, comparison, or performance, they often deliver short-term highs and long-term emptiness.

The most dangerous goals are the ones that win you applause but drain your spirit.

Most of us were taught to set goals from a place of pressure or comparison. To prove something. To stay relevant. To catch up. To outrun fear.

And so, we achieve—but feel misaligned. We accomplish—but do not arrive. Why? Because we have confused movement with meaning.

This chapter is about reclaiming the deeper purpose of goal setting. Not to abandon goals, but to anchor them. To move from autopilot to intention. From striving to soul.

You do not have to give up your ambition. But you do have to give up the illusion that every goal worth pursuing lives on someone else's scoreboard.

Here, we begin a new practice. One where the goal is not just to succeed—but to feel something true along the way.

One where achievement becomes an expression of alignment, not a desperate grasp for it.

Welcome to goal setting that begins with soul—and ends with fulfillment.

The Problem with Surface-Level Goals

Most of us have been taught to set goals that are easy to quantify and easy to admire. They are the kind of goals you can post about. Talk about. Measure on a spreadsheet.

- "I want to make more money."
- "I want to lose weight."
- "I want a bigger house."

These goals sound productive. Responsible. Aspirational. But when you pause and ask *why*, something deeper starts to surface.

- "Because I'll feel more secure."
- "Because I want to be loved."
- "Because then I'll feel successful."

Suddenly, the conversation shifts. You are no longer talking about money or weight or square footage. You are talking about belonging. Safety. Worthiness.

These goals are not wrong. They are just incomplete. *They point to deeper unmet needs that we have not yet named.* Because without awareness, we end up chasing symbols of fulfillment instead of the real thing.

A high income might symbolize security. A fit body might symbolize love or self-respect. A big house might symbolize status or arrival.

But the symbol is not the substance.

And when the symbol is all we chase—without understanding the need underneath—we arrive at our goals only to discover we are still hungry. Still searching. Still hoping that the next milestone will finally make us feel whole.

That is the danger of surface-level goals. They look good on paper, but they leave your soul out of the equation.

They create a life that appears successful from the outside—but feels strangely hollow on the inside.

That is why the first step toward fulfillment is not bigger goals. It is braver questions.

Because when you skip the soul work, you do not just risk disappointment—you risk building a life that does not actually fit the shape of your spirit.

From External Metrics to Internal Meaning

If surface-level goals lead us astray, the solution is not to stop setting goals. It is to start setting better ones—goals that are rooted in meaning, not just metrics.

Too often, we begin with the question:

• What do I want to achieve?

But a better question—the one that shifts everything—is this:

• How do I want to feel?

That is not a soft question. It is a clarifying one. Because it cuts through noise. It bypasses ego. It gets to the core of what actually matters.

Start there, and you may realize something surprising. The six-figure month is not about money—it is about freedom. The perfect body is not about abs—it is about vitality. The big house is not about space—it is about feeling rooted. The personal brand is not about followers—it is about being seen.

And once you know the feeling you are truly after, you can ask the most important question of all.

Is this the **most aligned** way to feel it?

Goals are not just tasks. They are threads in the story of who you are becoming. And the most fulfilling goals are the ones that make that story feel honest, coherent, and deeply your own.

When we fixate on outcomes, we lose connection to the process. We stop asking if this path still nourishes us—and start chasing the finish line, even if it leads us further from ourselves.

Because sometimes, the thing we are chasing is not the only—or even the best—way to feel what we crave.

Want *peace?*

Maybe the real goal is not scaling your business—it is simplifying your life.

Want *connection?*

Maybe it is not about building a brand—it is about deepening your relationships.

Want *vitality?*

Maybe it is not about the perfect physique—but about consistent, nourishing rhythms that energize you.

Want *freedom?*

Maybe it is not about quitting your job—it is about rewriting your relationship to time.

Want *joy?*

Maybe it is not about arrival at all—but about noticing the beauty already around you.

The key insight is this: When you lead with *feeling*, achievement becomes an expression of truth—not a substitute for it. You stop chasing goals that look good and start building a life that feels good.

From the inside out.

The Soul-Aligned Goal Filter

Not every **goal** deserves your energy.

Once you begin identifying the feelings beneath your goals, a new kind of discernment becomes possible. You stop setting goals reactively—and start choosing them intentionally.

That is where the Soul-Aligned Goal Filter comes in.

Before you pour time, energy, and identity into any ambition, pause. Ask yourself five questions. Let them be your compass—not to tell you *what* to pursue, but to help you understand *why* you are pursuing it.

1. Does this goal reflect who I am becoming— or who I am trying not to disappoint?

Sometimes, we chase goals that belong to an outdated version of us—or worse, to someone else entirely.

This question invites you to check for alignment with your current evolution, not your past expectations or others' projections.

2. Will this goal energize me—or just impress others?

The most dangerous goals are the ones that win you applause but drain your spirit.

There is nothing wrong with external recognition—but it should be a byproduct, not a requirement.

3. What feeling am I chasing with this goal—and is there a simpler, more soul-aligned way to experience it now?

Often, we take the long route to something that is available now. Why spend a year chasing something you could give yourself today in a quieter, more authentic way?

4. If I achieve it, will I feel aligned—or just relieved?

Relief might mean you have been chasing out of fear, not purpose.

Alignment feels different—it expands you. It integrates you.

5. Am I willing to enjoy theprocess—not just the prize?

Soul-aligned goals invite you into the journey. Even when it is hard, you find meaning in the steps—not just the outcome.

If you cannot imagine enjoying the process, ask whether it is truly your goal—or someone else's script.

These questions are not judgmental. They are discerning. Because the right goals do not pull you away from yourself—they draw you deeper in.

When a goal passes through this filter, what is left is clarity. Not just about *what* to pursue, but *how* to pursue it—without abandoning yourself in the process.

Because the goal is not just to achieve. It is to stay whole while doing it.

Goals That Do *NOT* Own You

There is a kind of goal that feels like a cage.

It starts with ambition—but somewhere along the way, it morphs into obligation.

What once lit you up begins to weigh you down. You stop moving toward the goal, and start being dragged by it.

That is what happens when goals are fueled by fear, comparison, or the need to prove. They do not just ask for your effort—they demand your identity. And slowly, they begin to own you.

But there is another way.

Goals with soul are expansive—not exhausting.

They invite your full presence, not your constant pressure. They stretch you toward who you are becoming—but never away from who you are.

You still work hard. You still show up. But the striving does not feel frantic. It feels focused. You are not chasing your worth—you are expressing it.

The difference is in the *relationship*.

When a goal owns you, you become reactive. Trapped in all-or-nothing thinking. Obsessed with outcomes.

But when you own the goal, you stay grounded. You can pivot without shame. Rest without guilt.

You can honor progress without needing perfection.

You do not need to abandon ambition to protect your peace. You just need to choose goals that do not require you to betray yourself.

Because the right goals do not consume you. They *clarify* you.

And that is how you know you are on the path of fulfillment—not just performance.

Practices for Soul-Aligned Goal Setting

Because soul-aligned goals
are not just chosen once—
they are **revisited, reconnected,
and renewed.**

Once you begin setting goals that reflect your values and desired feelings, the work does not stop there. In fact, that is when the deeper work begins.

Soulful goals do not thrive in hustle culture. They thrive in rhythm. In reflection. In the kind of intentional space where alignment is not a one-time act, but a living practice.

Strategic pauses—like quarterly reflections or monthly check-ins—are not indulgent. They are protective. They help you prevent goal fatigue and keep your ambition grounded in your evolving truth.

Here are a few rituals and tools to help you stay aligned—not just with what you want, but with *why* you want it.

1. Annual Vision Ritual

A day to disconnect from noise—and reconnect with your inner compass.

Once a year, step away from your routine. Leave the inbox behind. Get quiet enough to hear what your deeper self is asking for. Spend time journaling, walking, dreaming, and asking:

- Who am I becoming?
- What truly matters this year?
- What am I being called to create—not just accomplish?

This is not a planning session. It is a re-alignment ceremony.

2. Quarterly Soul Check-In

A reminder that goals are not contracts—they are conversations.

Every 90 days, revisit your goals. Not to assess progress in metrics alone—but to check for soul alignment. Ask:

- Are these goals still mine?
- Do they still reflect the person I am growing into?
- What needs to be released, revised, or recommitted to?

This keeps you agile. Honest. Grounded. Because staying true to your goals is less important than staying true to yourself.

3. Reverse Goal Mapping

Start with the feeling—not the finish line.

Instead of jumping to the what, begin with the why you want to feel what you want to feel. Ask:

- How do I want to feel this year?
- What environments, relationships, and daily habits support that feeling?
- What kinds of goals naturally emerge from that emotional foundation?

Let the feeling lead—and let the form follow.

4. Monthly Micro-Actions

Tiny steps, soul-aligned.

Each month, choose one small action that honors your deeper values. Not because it will radically change your life overnight—but because it keeps you moving in the right direction, with integrity.

Big goals are often achieved through humble, consistent acts. Especially the ones that begin in stillness.

These practices are not rigid systems—they are invitations.
- To pause.
- To listen.
- To realign with the person you are becoming—over and over again.

Because soul-aligned goals are not set and forgotten. They are tended to, like a garden. And the more you return to that soil, the more naturally they grow.

Reflection Prompts

Questions not for your to-do list—but for your truth.

The beauty of soul-aligned goals is that they do not start with action. They start with awareness.

Before you commit to another milestone, pause. Turn inward. Ask yourself the following questions. Not from the mind alone, but from the heart and gut:

Which of my current goals feel heavy or forced?

These are the goals that take more energy to justify than to pursue. The ones you keep trying to convince yourself are right—because they once were, or because they sound impressive, or because someone else expects them.

Notice where you feel tension, dread, or emotional fatigue.

What would it mean to *release* that goal—or reshape it into something that feels more true?

Which goals light me up—even if they scare me?

Not all fear is a red flag. Sometimes, it is the signal of something meaningful. A stretch. A leap. A calling.

What are the goals that stir something real in you—something tender, alive, and maybe a little wild?

Pay attention. These are often the ones worth honoring, even if they do not come with guarantees.

What is one goal I could set today that reflects my soul—not my stress?

You do not need a five-year plan. You just need one next move that feels aligned.

What is one goal—small or bold—that reflects your values, your truth, your becoming? Not because it is strategic. Not because it is expected. But because it feels *right*.

These are not quick journaling prompts. They are doorways—into deeper clarity.

Let them take time. Let them sit with you. And when you are ready, let them speak back to you—not with noise, but with knowing.

Closing Thought

- You do not need fewer goals.
- You need truer goals.

Goals that reflect your values, not just your velocity. That help you grow in wholeness, not just in visibility. That feel honest in process, not just impressive in outcome.

Because fulfillment does not come from how much you achieve. It comes from how deeply your goals align with the person you are becoming.

- Set fewer goals that deplete you.
- Set more goals that return you to yourself.

The point of setting goals is not to prove your worth. It is to express your truth. To move through the world with clarity, not performance. With presence, not pressure.

When your goals reflect your deepest self—your values, your vision, your voice—then success is no longer just an external achievement. It becomes a daily embodiment. A way of walking through life with purpose, integrity, and peace.

Because fulfillment is not waiting at the finish line. It is present in every step you take that honors who you are becoming.

So set your goals. But set them from the inside out.

- Let them stretch you—but never sever you.
- Let them challenge you—but never consume you.

And as you walk your path—one soul-aligned step at a time—remember this:

- You are not here to chase.
- You are here to choose.

And every goal you choose with soul… becomes a way home.

8

Growth can be peaceful, not just painful. Learn to expand without burning out.

Choosing Growth Over Grind

*W*e are praised for pushing.

For staying late, grinding harder, and never letting up.

We admire the striver. We celebrate the unrelenting. And somewhere along the way, we begin to confuse effort with identity.

You keep climbing. Because everyone else is climbing. Because the summit always seems just a little higher. Because somewhere in the distance, success is waiting—and maybe peace is with it.

But what happens when the climb becomes the point, not the path? What happens when movement becomes compulsion? When you no longer know who you are without the pace?

This is the hidden danger of the grind.

It does not just take your energy. It takes your presence. Your softness. Your joy.

We are told growth is supposed to hurt. That success demands sacrifice.

But what if that is only part of the truth?

What if growth could be spacious? What if progress did not have to come with pressure? What if you could evolve—and still feel whole?

This chapter is an invitation to grow differently. To stop measuring your life by output and start honoring it through alignment. To trade the grind for something richer: *rooted growth.*

Rhythmic expansion. A life that rises without unraveling you.

Let's begin.

You Were not Made to Burn Out

The hustle culture anthem is loud—and deeply familiar:

- Rise and grind.
- Outwork everyone.
- Sleep is for the weak.
- No pain, no gain.

At first, it sounds like courage. Like discipline. Like drive.

And in the beginning, it even works.

You push harder. Move faster. Stay later. You stack wins. Hit goals. Garner praise.

- You feel productive.
- You feel important.
- You feel—ironically—in control.

But what you do not feel is *yourself.*

Because slowly, without warning, the rhythm starts to take more than it gives. You begin to sacrifice sleep for output, relationships for revenue, stillness for stimulation.

The things that once felt energizing now feel obligatory. Your days blur. Your creativity dulls. Your body stiffens. Your soul retreats.

And one day, in a rare moment of quiet honesty, you see it: You have been growing—but not *living.*

You have been advancing—but not aligning. Accumulating accomplishments but drifting further from the very self those accomplishments were supposed to fulfill.

This is the quiet tragedy of burnout. Not that you are weak, but that you have been strong in the wrong direction for too long.

Burnout is not just fatigue—it is the erosion of meaning. A signal that your growth may have lost its grounding.

We were not made to burn out. We were made to *build.* To *create.* To *contribute.*

But also to *rest.* To *feel.* To *be.*

The question, then, is not whether to grow—but *how.*

Will you grow through pressure and depletion?

Or through presence and alignment?

True growth expands from within—it is the expression of becoming, not the fear of being left behind.

This chapter is about shifting from grind to grounded growth. From output at all costs… to effort that honors your humanity.

Because sustainable growth is not about how much you can squeeze from yourself.

It is about how deeply you can stay rooted in yourself—*even as you rise*.

The Lie of the Grind

The grind sells us a powerful myth.

It tells us that *rest is something you earn*—a luxury reserved for the finish line, once you have proved yourself through sweat, sacrifice, and sleepless nights.

But the truth is, *real growth requires rest.*

Not as a retreat from progress, but as its partner.

Rest is not the opposite of effort. It is the foundation of clarity, renewal, and resilience.

It restores creativity, nurtures innovation, and builds the capacity for long-term sustainability.

The grind tells us that *pressure creates diamonds*—as if human beings were meant to endure relentless compression. But pressure does not just create. It can *crush*.

It can strip joy from the journey. It can disconnect you from your body, your values, your relationships.

It can convince you that burnout is a badge of honor.

The grind tells us that *pain means progress*. But that is only part of the story.

Yes, discomfort can be a teacher. But so can *joy*. So can *curiosity*. So can *flow*, *ease*, and *alignment*.

You do not have to suffer your way into success. You do not have to prove your worth through depletion.

Here is the shift.

Grind is external pressure. Growth is internal expansion.

Grind says *push harder*. Growth says *listen deeper*.

Grind is performative. Growth is transformative.

Grind is rooted in fear—of falling behind, of not being enough. Growth is rooted in *trust*—that who you are becoming matters more than how fast you get there.

So maybe it is time to stop glorifying exhaustion. To stop worshiping the grind as proof of your commitment.

And instead—start honoring *alignment* as the truest expression of your power.

Because when your growth comes from within, you do not just *rise*— you *rise whole*.

Redefining What Growth Looks Like

We have inherited a narrow image of what growth should look like.

It is often loud. Fast. Public.

It shows up in big leaps, viral wins, packed calendars, and perfect morning routines.

129

It is measured in milestones and applauded when it is visible.

But real growth—sustainable, soul-aligned growth—is not always so cinematic.

Sometimes growth looks like *slowing down* when every instinct tells you to speed up. Sometimes it looks like *saying no* to an opportunity that flatters your ego but drains your energy. Sometimes it looks like *getting quiet*—not because you have lost your fire, but because you are tending to the deeper roots of it.

Growth is not always a straight line.

It rarely comes with a highlight reel or a neatly framed success story. Sometimes, it happens quietly—beneath the surface, far from anyone's applause.

Sometimes, it looks like stillness. Sometimes, it feels like unraveling. Sometimes, it is hidden in the unseen work of healing, letting go, recalibrating.

Because growth is not just about moving forward. It is about moving *truthfully*.

You may not be sprinting. But you are learning to move with intention.

You may not be winning in obvious ways. But you are learning to live in *alignment*.

You may not be checking off every box. But you are learning which boxes matter—and which were never yours to carry.

When we redefine what growth looks like, we stop measuring it by speed and start measuring it by substance. By integrity. By how deeply we are becoming the person we are here to be—not just how much we are producing along the way.

So the next time you find yourself doubting your progress because it is not flashy, fast, or publicly validated, remember: Quiet growth is still growth.

Restful growth is still growth.

Messy, nonlinear, soul-driven growth is not lesser. It is often *truer*.

And in this redefinition lies your power. The power to grow *without grinding yourself down*. The power to rise in a way that reflects—not rejects—your inner truth.

What Sustainable Growth Looks Like

Growth that costs you your wholeness is not growth—it is erosion.

Sustainable growth respects your energy, your seasons, and your truth. Here is what it looks like:

- It is not always linear.
- It is not always visible.
- It is not always fast.

But it is always rooted.

You still stretch—but you do so from strength, not strain. You still rise—but you do so with rest, not rigidity.

Growth is not just about motion. It is about rhythm.

Energy alignment is how we build something that lasts without breaking ourselves in the process.

Sustainable growth expands your capacity without compromising your core.

It invites discipline, yes—but not desperation.

It leaves room for rest, curiosity, creativity.

You move from urgency to intentionality.

From proving to becoming.

This is how you grow with grace.

After redefining what growth means, we can begin to recognize what sustainable growth actually feels like.

It is not the frantic pace of constant striving. It is the grounded, intentional unfolding of becoming.

Here is what that kind of growth looks like in practice.

1. Aligned with your energy

You work with your rhythms—not against them.

You stop seeing exhaustion as a badge of honor and start listening to the wisdom of your body.

You recognize that some seasons are for planting, others for harvesting, and still others for rest—and that each is essential.

Your effort becomes smarter, not just harder.

2. Integrated with your life

Your goals do not compete with your relationships, health, or peace.

You no longer pursue success in one area by sacrificing wholeness in another.

You do not compartmentalize your life into work *versus* everything else—you let it all support the same truth.

Growth becomes part of a life that feels cohesive, not chaotic.

3. Paced for longevity

You plan not just for this month—but for the next decade.

You stop sprinting toward urgency and begin investing in endurance. You ask: *What would it look like to grow in a way I can sustain—not just survive?*

You make space for pauses, course corrections, and evolution—knowing that meaningful growth is a marathon, not a fire drill.

4. Connected to joy

You leave room for curiosity, beauty, wonder, and rest—not just productivity.

You remind yourself that joy is not a distraction from progress—it is a sign you are on a path worth walking.

You let lightness in, not because life is easy, but because your spirit needs nourishment too.

If you cannot enjoy the journey, the destination will not save you.

Because the arrival moment is fleeting. But how you travel—the pace, the presence, the peace—that is what becomes your life.

The Seasons of Growth

Nature does not bloom year-round. Neither should you.

We know this intuitively. We see it in the trees, the tides, the arc of the sun. Nature thrives not by constant expansion, but by honoring rhythm, rest, and renewal.

And yet, we so often expect ourselves to be in perpetual bloom. Always producing. Always achieving. Always *on*.

But just like nature, your growth has seasons—each with its own wisdom, purpose, and pace.

Planting *(visioning and dreaming)*

This is the quiet beginning. A time of imagination, intention, and the courage to hope.

You may not see visible results yet—but under the surface, deep alignment is taking root.

Growing *(focused effort and momentum)*

Here comes action. Forward motion. The sprouting of the seeds you have sown. This is where energy flows freely—when you are aligned, engaged, and fueled by purpose. But even in this season, growth is not frantic. It is focused.

Pruning *(letting go of what is no longer working)*

To grow wisely is to release what no longer serves.

This is the season of refinement—cutting back distractions, old identities, outdated goals.

It can feel like loss, but it is actually a return to clarity.

Pruning is not a setback. It is sacred editing.

Resting *(integration, recovery, stillness)*

Just as winter nourishes the soil, rest restores your soul.

This season often gets mistaken for stagnation—but in truth, it is where depth is formed.

Integration happens here. Renewal happens here. Vision is reborn here.

Stillness is not the absence of growth—it is the soil of it.

Sustainable growth is not about pushing through every season.
It is about honoring the one you are in.

When you stop resisting your season—when you let go of the pressure to always be "on"—you begin to grow in a way that is not only more peaceful, but more powerful.

Ask yourself:

- What season am I in right now?
- And what would it look like to honor that—fully, without guilt?

Because trying to bloom in winter will not make the flowers come faster. But trusting the rhythm will make them richer when they do.

The Growth Season Wheel
Honoring Your Natural Rhythms of Expansion

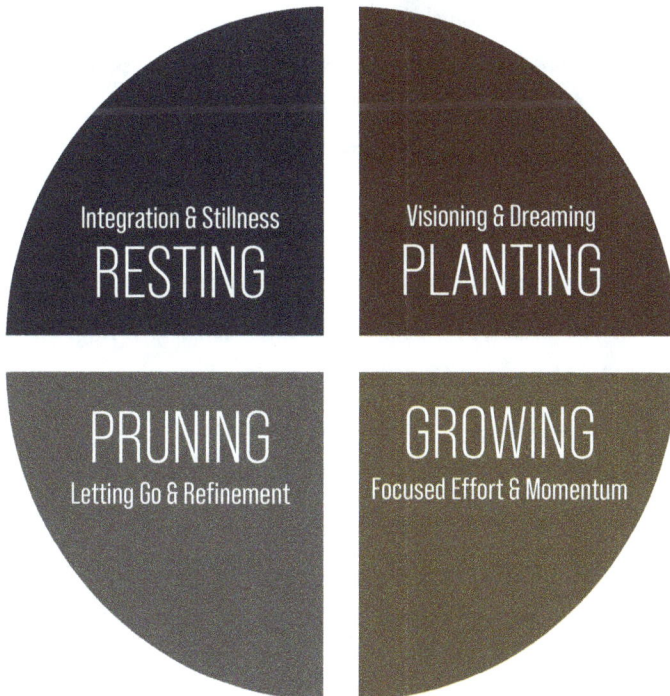

Integration & Stillness
RESTING

Visioning & Dreaming
PLANTING

PRUNING
Letting Go & Refinement

GROWING
Focused Effort & Momentum

Releasing the Need to Prove

Because your worth is not up for negotiation.

For many of us, grind is not just a work habit—it is a coping mechanism. We push harder, stay later, do more—not out of purpose, but out of fear. Fear of being seen as lazy. Fear of falling behind. Fear of not being enough unless we have something to show for it.

Grind often comes from insecurity—the quiet, unspoken belief that we must *earn* our value. That worthiness is conditional. That if we just do enough, produce enough, achieve enough… we will finally feel safe.

Respected.

Seen.

But when you begin to operate from a place of *inherent worthiness*, something fundamental shifts.

- You no longer move from fear—you move from alignment.
- You do not chase validation—you live in expression.
- You do not grind to prove you belong—you grow because something inside you is ready to evolve.

This is the difference between performance and purpose. Between exhausting yourself for applause and expanding yourself from truth.

When you know you are already enough, you stop trying to become someone else's definition of it.

- You still strive. But it is no longer frantic.
- You still stretch. But it is no longer out of lack.

You grow because it feels right—not because you are afraid of what happens if you do not. And that changes everything.

Because the moment you stop trying to *earn* your worth, you finally begin to *embody* it.

Daily Questions to Stay in Growth, Not Grind

Because how you move through the day is how you shape your life.

It is easy to slip back into the old patterns. Even after redefining growth and releasing the grind, the world around you still rewards speed, urgency, and output.

That is why staying rooted in sustainable, soul-aligned growth requires not just intention—but daily inquiry.

These questions are not tasks. They are tuning forks. They help you check your resonance before you act—so your energy, choices, and effort remain in harmony with who you are becoming.

What would it look like to grow with ease today?

This question interrupts the reflex to push. It invites you to find power in gentleness. It does not mean avoiding effort—it means choosing effort that supports you, rather than depleting you.

Am I forcing something—or flowing with it?

Force is often a sign of misalignment. Flow does not mean easy—but it does mean congruent. This question helps you notice where you are gripping too tightly, and where a lighter touch might serve you better.

What is one thing I can release to reclaim my energy?

Every day, you carry things that were never meant to be permanent: outdated goals, inherited expectations, unnecessary pressure. This question helps you let go of what drains you—so you have more space for what nourishes you.

Is this action aligned with the person I want to become?

This is the compass question. It brings you back to your larger vision—not of achievement, but of embodiment. It helps you filter your to-do list through the lens of *becoming*, not just completing.

These questions are not about being perfect. They are about being present.

Because when you ask better questions, you make better decisions—decisions that build a life of sustainable growth, grounded power, and real fulfillment.

Reflection Prompts

Because awareness is where transformation begins.

Sustainable growth does not happen by accident. It happens when we pause long enough to notice:

- Where am I moving from intention… and where am I just reacting?
- Where am I honoring my energy… and where am I overriding it?

These questions are not here to fix you. They are here to *center you*. To help you shift from autopilot into alignment—from grind into growth.

Take your time with these. Let them sink beneath the surface.

Where am I grinding out of fear or pressure?

Look for the places where urgency is driving you more than clarity. Where you feel the need to prove, to keep up, to not disappoint. These are often the areas where you are outsourcing your sense of worth.

What part of my life is calling for a slower, deeper kind of growth?

Not all growth is upward. Sometimes, you are being called to grow downward—into deeper roots. Into maturity, presence, healing, or stillness. This is the growth that does not make headlines—but makes you.

How can I build in more restoration without losing momentum?

This is not about stopping. It is about pacing. Nourishing. Tending to your capacity so you can sustain what you are creating.

Ask: **What rhythms restore me?**

Because real momentum is built on rhythms that last—not sprints that burn out.

These reflections do not need immediate answers. Let them open a conversation with your deeper self. The kind of conversation that leads not just to achievement—but to *wholeness*.

The Grind-To-Growth Shift Map

From Grind	To Growth
Proving Worth through Output	Expressing Truth through Alignment
Urgency and Pressure	Purposeful Pace and Presence
Exhaustion as a Badge of Honor	Rest as a Source of Strength
Pushing Past Limits	Honoring Natural Rhythms
Fear-Driven Action	Intention-Led Choices
Linear, Nonstop Productivity	Seasonal, Sustainable Cycles
External Validation	Internal Clarity and Self-Trust

From Grind to Grounding

A 2-Minute Meditation to Return to Yourself

Close your eyes. Take a slow, deep breath.

Let the tension soften from your jaw.
Let your shoulders drop just a little more.
Let your breath settle into its natural rhythm.

Now, ask yourself—gently, without judgment:

Where am I forcing something today?
What would it feel like to release it—just for this moment?

Notice the part of you that is tired.
Notice the part of you that is still reaching, striving, pushing.

Now imagine that part being held—not driven.
Supported—not squeezed.
Respected—not rushed.

Let yourself arrive here.

Just here.

Just now.

And remember:

You are not behind.

You are not late.

You are not your output.

You are enough—right here, breathing, becoming.

Closing Thought

You do not have to burn yourself down to build a beautiful life.

That is the lie the grind tells you: that only through exhaustion comes excellence. That depletion is a necessary price for significance.

But you know better now.

You were never meant to be a machine.

You were meant to be a living, breathing, evolving being—capable of deep presence, rich creativity, and lasting contribution.

Growth does not have to grind you down to be real. It can be honest. Spacious. Rhythmic.

It can support your soul, not just your schedule.

Because the most sustainable growth is not the loudest. It is the kind that strengthens you at the roots—so you can rise without losing yourself.

So, choose growth that nourishes you. Growth that is not rooted in fear, but in *wholeness*. Growth that breathes. That bends. That listens to your seasons and trusts your timing.

Growth that lasts—not just because it is efficient, but because it is *aligned*.

Because a rich life is not built in a frenzy. It is cultivated—with care, with clarity, and with courage.

And when your growth reflects your truth, you do not have to prove anything.

You simply become.

9

CHAPTER NINE

A Practical
Guide to
Living Aligned.

The Fulfillment Framework

By now, you have unpacked the hidden trade-offs of success. You have questioned the myth that achievement guarantees peace. You have seen the drift that happens when ambition outruns alignment.

This chapter is where it all begins to shift—where reflection becomes structure, and clarity becomes a way of life. Because fulfillment is not just something you feel. It is something you build—on purpose, over time, and with the right tools.

THE
FULLFILLMENT
curve

Turning Insight into Structure

You have likely felt the tension: the quiet dissonance between what
the world rewards and what your soul is asking for. You have seen
how easy it is to get caught in the rhythm of chasing—more goals,
more progress, more success—only to find yourself further from a
sense of peace.

You have also begun to see that more is not the same as meaningful. That achievement, while valuable, does not always leave you
feeling whole. And that even success, when misaligned, can feel
strangely hollow.

This chapter is where it all begins to take shape.

Because insight is powerful—but without structure, it drifts.

And reflection is essential—but without direction, it loops.

What you need now is a framework.

Not a formula.

Not another goal-setting method.

But a grounded, repeatable way to live aligned—with your energy,
your values, and the life you truly want to build.

That is the purpose of this chapter: to offer a compass for your
fulfillment. To give shape to your intuition. To turn what you have
learned into how you live.

We will walk through a system designed not to prescribe your
path, but to help you listen more clearly to it—and stay on course,
even as life changes.

This framework functions like a compass—anchored in clarity
and choice. Like tools used in ACT (Acceptance and Commitment

Therapy), it does not remove uncertainty. It helps you navigate it with integrity.

This is the bridge between insight and integration. Between clarity and choice. Between intention and embodiment.

Let's begin.

The Four Components of the Fulfillment Framework
A System for Clarity, Alignment, and Intentional Growth

Fulfillment is not a mystery. It is not something you stumble upon by accident or achieve once and for all. It is the result of living with alignment—between who you are, what you value, and how you move through the world.

> But alignment requires **awareness.**
> And awareness requires **structure.**

That is where the Fulfillment Framework comes in.

This is more than a reflection tool—it is a living system. A way to pause, check in, and course-correct with intention. It is designed to help you make decisions that are not just smart or strategic, but *soulful.*

It does not promise certainty. But it *does* promise clarity—if you are willing to be honest.

The framework is built on *four integrated components.* Each plays a specific role in helping you notice when you are in alignment—and when you are drifting from yourself.

Together, they form a cycle you can return to anytime you feel off-track, overextended, or unsure of what comes next.

The Four Components:

1. The Rich Life Filter™

The first pause. The deeper question.

Before you commit to anything—a new project, a next step, a life decision—this is your first check-in.

It helps you ask:

"Does this serve the life I actually want—or just the one I am performing?"

The Rich Life Filter™ does not offer answers. It clears the fog. It gets you honest, fast. It strips away ego, external pressure, and empty obligations. It is how you begin with intention—so you do not spend months chasing something that was never yours to begin with.

2. The Alignment Audit

The core evaluation: Meaning, Energy, Sustainability.

Once you have passed through the filter, it is time to assess the path you are on. This is where you rate your current project, pursuit, or pattern using three internal metrics:

Meaning – Does this align with what I value most?

Energy – Does this give more than it takes?

Sustainability – Can I keep doing this without losing myself?

This audit reveals the *quality* of your path—not just its momentum.

3. The Fulfillment Score

The measurement—not of success, but of presence.

This is where you assign a score to each lens (1–10), not to perform, but to reflect. It creates a snapshot of your current alignment. Sometimes, you will be surprised. A path that looks perfect on paper might feel empty inside. That dissonance is the data. And it matters.

The Fulfillment Score helps you name what you already feel—and make better choices from it.

4. The Recalibration Practice

The rhythm that keeps you aligned.

Fulfillment is not static. Life changes. You change. That is why this is not a one-time process—it is a rhythm of checking in.

- Monthly, for high performers.
- Quarterly, for intentional life design.
- Annually, for big-picture direction.

It is a ritual of awareness. A return to yourself. A reminder that you always have the ability to adjust, realign, and re-choose—without guilt.

These four components do not exist in isolation. They work together, forming a system that helps you stay close to what matters most. The Rich Life Filter™ points you inward. The Alignment Audit reveals what is true. The Fulfillment Score gives you feedback. And the Recalibration Practice ensures you keep evolving with clarity and care.

This is how fulfillment becomes *practice*, not just philosophy.

Let's go deeper.

Deep Dive – The Alignment Audit
The Inner Metrics That Matter Most

Once you have used the Rich Life Filter™ to clear the fog and get honest about what you are considering, the next step is to go deeper.

That is where the Alignment Audit comes in.

This is the heart of the Fulfillment Framework—the part where you assess whether the path you are on *feels* right, not just *looks* right. It helps you evaluate your alignment through three essential lenses: *Meaning, Energy,* and *Sustainability.*

- Each one is a form of internal feedback.
- Each one points to a different dimension of fulfillment.

Together, they offer a grounded, multidimensional view of whether the life you are building is actually supporting the life you want.

1. Meaning – Does it matter?

Fulfillment begins with meaning. Without it, even the most polished achievements feel hollow. You can build the dream, earn the title, reach the milestone—and still feel like something is missing.

That "something" is often meaning.

Ask yourself:

- Is this aligned with my core values?
- Does it contribute to the person I want to become?
- Is it connected to a purpose larger than ego or comparison?

This is not about grand gestures or lofty missions. It is about honest alignment. If something holds no personal resonance, it might still offer short-term rewards—money, status, validation—but those fade fast.

- Meaning is what roots you.

- It is what stays when the novelty wears off.

- It is what makes the process feel worthwhile—even on hard days.

In a noisy world full of borrowed goals and external noise, meaning is what brings you home.

2. Energy – Does it energize or deplete me?

Energy is your internal signal system. It is how your body and spirit let you know whether you are in alignment.

Ask:

- Do I feel alive when I do this work—or exhausted?

- Is the process life-giving or soul-sucking?

- Do I look forward to this—or dread it?

Let's be clear:
fulfillment does not mean effortless.

Deep, meaningful work often requires effort. But there is a critical difference between effort that fuels you—and effort that erodes you.

When you are energized, even hard work can feel expansive. When you are depleted, even small tasks feel like a burden.

- Energy is information.

- Listen to it.

When you consistently feel drained, even by things that "should" feel good, it is not a failure—it is a signal.

3. Sustainability – Can I keep doing this and still feel whole?

You can be on a path that is meaningful and energizing—and still burn out if it is not sustainable.

A fulfilling life is not just about what you do. It is about how well you can *continue* doing it while honoring your health, your relationships, and your peace of mind. Ask:

- Is this lifestyle, pace, or process sustainable for me?
- Am I sacrificing essential parts of myself to maintain this path?
- What would need to shift for this to be more easeful?
- Sustainability is not weakness.
- It is wisdom.

If your version of success requires trading away your well-being, it is not success—it is self-abandonment dressed up as achievement.

Sustainability is about creating a rhythm that supports growth *and* renewal. It is how you build momentum without losing yourself in the process.

The Power of All Three

When *Meaning, Energy,* and *Sustainability* are present, you are likely in a high-fulfillment zone. When one is missing, misalignment is already underway. And when all three are low—it is time to rethink the path entirely.

This audit does not judge you. It guides you.

It shows you where to go deeper, what to question, and how to adjust with grace. Because fulfillment is not static. It evolves with you. And you are allowed to change your path when the person walking it changes.

How to Use the Framework
A Repeatable Process for Realignment

The Fulfillment Framework is not something you use once and forget. It is a living tool—a structure you return to when life feels out of sync, when the next step feels unclear, or when you are doing "all the right things" but feel strangely disconnected.

This is your compass.

Not to tell you where to go, but to help you make sure the direction you are heading still feels true.

The process unfolds in four steps; each tied to one of the framework's components. You can move through all of them in a single journaling session or revisit them separately as needed.

Step 1: Filter for Truth
(The Rich Life Filter™)

Before you assess anything, pause. Ask the deeper question:

"Does this serve the life I actually want—
or just the one I am performing?"

If the answer feels unclear, that is your first insight.

The Rich Life Filter™ is your signal to slow down. To strip away what looks good but feels off. To reconnect with what actually matters before you pour more energy into the wrong pursuit.

Use it before saying yes. Use it when you are tempted to default.

It is not a gatekeeper. It is a clarifier.

Step 2: Audit for Alignment
(The Alignment Audit)

Now that you have filtered out the noise, it is time to evaluate what remains.

Choose a project, opportunity, habit, or decision you want to examine. Then rate it in each of the following categories, using a 1–10 scale:

Meaning – Does this reflect my values and purpose?

Energy – Does this make me feel alive and engaged?

Sustainability – Can I keep doing this without sacrificing my well-being?

Take your time. Do not score for perfection. Score for truth.

This is not about impressing anyone—not even yourself.

It is about becoming more honest with what you already know.

Step 3: Reflect with Honesty

(The Fulfillment Score)

Now look at your numbers. This is your snapshot.

If all three scores are **7 or above**: You are likely on a high-fulfillment path. Stay the course. Deepen your engagement. This is a season to invest and expand.

If one or two scores are **5 or below**: Something is off. It may not require quitting—but it does require *recalibration*.

Ask:

• Can the work be reframed to connect with deeper meaning?

• Can you shift the process to protect your energy?

• Can something be simplified to make it more sustainable?

If all three scores are **4 or below**: This is a red flag. The path you are on may no longer support who you are becoming. This does not mean failure. It means evolution. Letting go may be the most aligned thing you can do.

Your Fulfillment Score is not a verdict. It is an invitation—to realign, redirect, or recommit.

Step 4: Revisit with Rhythm

(The Recalibration Practice)

Fulfillment is not a destination. It is a dynamic relationship with your values, your capacity, and your season of life.

What lit you up last year may not serve you today.

What energized you in your 30s might feel draining in your 50s.

This is normal. This is growth.

That is why recalibration is not an emergency protocol—it is a regular practice.

Suggested cadence:

Monthly – For high performers navigating frequent decisions

Quarterly – For intentional life design and course-correction

Annually – For deep reflection and long-range clarity

Build it into your calendar like you would any other priority. Not to fix yourself—but to stay connected to yourself.

This framework does not require hours of journaling or radical reinvention. Often, a 15-minute pause and three honest scores are enough to shift the way you show up.

The goal is not to optimize every part of your life. It is to make sure the life you are building still feels like it is *yours*.

The Fulfillment Score vs. The Achievement Score

Two Metrics. Two Truths. One Life.

There is nothing wrong with achievement.

Setting goals. Measuring progress. Hitting milestones. Those things matter—because they help you grow, stay focused, and move forward.

But if achievement is your only measure of success, it is easy to win on paper and still feel lost inside.

That is where the Fulfillment Score comes in.

This tool does not replace your goals. It complements them. It holds space for your inner life—so you do not forget to measure what really matters while chasing what the world can see.

Achievement asks: Did I win?

- It is external.
- It measures outcomes, accolades, and progress.
- It shows up in trophies, metrics, promotions, dollars.

Fulfillment asks: Am I whole?

- It is internal.
- It measures alignment, integrity, and peace.
- It shows up in energy, presence, relationships, clarity.

You can have a high Achievement Score and a low Fulfillment Score.

You can crush your goals and still feel crushed by them.

That is not failure. That is misalignment.

The Fulfillment Score is a counterbalance. A corrective.

It reminds you to pause and ask:

- Am I doing this for approval or for truth?
- Is this goal still mine?
- Am I becoming someone I want to be— or just someone others admire?

Achievement vs. Fulfillment

A Simple Side-by-Side Reflection

Compare the success you achieved with the fulfillment you
felt, and reveal where they align—or fall apart.

Take a Recent Project, Role, or Milestone to Use Below:

Part One
The Achievement Score

Reflect on the external outcome:

What did you accomplish?

What was the visible result?

*On a scale of 1–10, how "successful"
was it by conventional standards?*

*What did you gain—financially,
professionally, socially?*

*How long did the satisfaction last?
What did it cost you?*

Your Achievement Score
[   ] /10

Part Two
The Fulfillment Score

Now go deeper:

Did this align with your core values?

Did it energize or drain you?

*Did it contribute to
something meaningful?*

*Did it make you feel proud
of how you showed up?*

*Would you choose this again,
knowing what you know now?*

Your Fulfillment Score
[   ] /10

Connect the Dots

Are your scores aligned—or is there a gap? What does that gap reveal?

*What would need to shift for your next goal to be
more fulfilling, not just more impressive?*

Insight Without Structure Loops

- *You can journal every day and still feel stuck.*

- *You can reflect on your goals and still repeat the same misalignments.*

- *Insight without structure can quickly dissolve into inertia.*

- *But when reflection is tethered to action—through a practice like this—it becomes a tool for alignment.*

- *This is why we build frameworks. Not to control our lives. But to clarify them.*

Fulfillment as Design Rhythm

- *The beauty of this framework is not in its complexity. It is in its repetition.*

- *Fulfillment is not a destination. It is a design rhythm. A way of relating to your own life with honesty, iteration, and grace.*

- *This framework gives you a language for your intuition. It turns your knowing into a navigational pattern.*

- *Not so you can perfect your life. But so you can inhabit it.*

- *Not so you never drift. But so you can return.*

- *You do not need more goals. You need better checkpoints.*

- *The Fulfillment Framework is how you begin to build a life that does not just look good on paper—but feels aligned in your bones.*

Examples in Practice

What Fulfillment Looks Like in Real Life

The Fulfillment Framework is not abstract. It is meant to be used—in the mess and movement of daily life.

These examples show how the same opportunity can feel very different depending on how it aligns with your values, energy, and capacity. They illustrate how fulfillment is never just about what you are doing but how and why you are doing it.

These snapshots invite you to filter, audit, and reflect.

Not to judge—but to notice. Not to fix—but to choose better.

Example 1: The Promotion

You are offered a major career advancement. A Bigger title. A Bigger paycheck. Much More prestige. It looks like the next logical step.

But when you pause for a second and apply the framework, something shifts.

The Rich Life Filter:

"This looks impressive—but is it still aligned with the life I want?" *The honest answer? Not entirely.*

Alignment Audit:

Meaning: 6 – It aligns with ambition, but not with evolving personal values.

Energy: 4 – The demands are draining. There is more pressure than inspiration.

Sustainability: 3 – It would require sacrificing time, peace, and relationships.

Fulfillment Score: 4.3 / 10

Interpretation: *This is a traditional "win" that may lead to quiet misalignment. It is not a no—but it might be a not this way. Consider negotiating terms, redefining what success means now, or finding ways to pursue advancement without losing yourself.*

Example 2: The Passion Project

You are working on something creative or deeply personal. It does not pay much—yet. There is no spotlight. But it feels like you.

The Rich Life Filter:

"This does not make sense to others—but it lights me up." *That is enough to keep going.*

Alignment Audit:

Meaning: 9 – It is rooted in your values and self-expression.

Energy: 9 – You feel alive when immersed in it.

Sustainability: 7 – It fits around your life, even if it takes planning.

Fulfillment Score: **8.3 / 10**

Interpretation: *This is high-fulfillment work. It may not yield immediate results, but it is worth pursuing. Trust that fulfillment compounds quietly— and that this kind of alignment often leads to outcomes you cannot yet predict.*

Example 3: The Side Hustle Burnout

What started as a creative outlet or income booster has become a burden. It no longer inspires—it exhausts.

The Rich Life Filter:

"I used to love this. Now I am doing it out of guilt and momentum." *That is the first red flag.*

Alignment Audit:

Meaning: 5 – It once had purpose but no longer feels connected.

Energy: 3 – You dread the work. It drains more than it gives.

Sustainability: 2 – It is eroding your rest, peace, and time.

Fulfillment Score: **3.3 / 10**

Interpretation: *It is time to pause. Let go. Reimagine. This chapter may be complete. Continuing risks burnout and disconnection. Release it with gratitude—and make room for something that aligns.*

Takeaway

These examples highlight a powerful truth: Not all "good" opportunities are good *for you*. And not all exits are failures—some are recalibrations.

The Fulfillment Framework helps you name what is true. It reminds you that success without self is hollow. And it gives you permission to choose from alignment—not just obligation.

Expanded Case Studies

How Fulfillment (and Misalignment) Show Up Everywhere

Fulfillment does not just live in your career.

It shows up in your relationships, your routines, your health, your parenting, your creative expression. And so does misalignment.

Below are real-life scenarios where the Fulfillment Framework can bring clarity. These examples are not about what is "right" or "wrong"—they are about noticing what is *real*. Each one shows how applying the framework helps you catch subtle drift before it becomes disconnection.

The Relationship That No Longer Fits

There is care, but less connection. There is history, but more heaviness than harmony. You are growing. They are not. You love them—but it feels like work, not warmth.

The Rich Life Filter:

"Am I holding on because it is aligned—or because it is familiar?" *Answer: Familiarity is leading.*

Alignment Audit:

Meaning: 5 – There is shared history, but it no longer reflects your values.

Energy: 4 – Conversations feel tense, not uplifting.

Sustainability: 3 – You are compromising peace to keep the connection alive.

Fulfillment Score: 4 / 10

Interpretation: *Time for honest reflection—or conversation. Some relationships are seasonal. Letting go does not erase love—it honors growth.*

Parenting Through a Major Transition

You are navigating divorce, a move, or job change—and still showing up for your kids. It is messy. You are stretched. But you are trying.

The Rich Life Filter:

"Am I being present in a way that reflects what I value?" *Yes—even in imperfection.*

Alignment Audit:

Meaning: 10 – This role is core to who you are.

Energy: 6 – Emotionally demanding, but purposeful.

Sustainability: 5 – Manageable, but just barely. You need support.

Fulfillment Score: 7 / 10

Interpretation: *You are in a hard season—not a misaligned one. You do not need perfection. You need presence—and small systems of care.*

The Fitness Regimen That has Become a Punishment

It started as self-care. Now it is control. The joy is gone. You are avoiding pain—but creating a new kind.

The Rich Life Filter:

"Am I moving for health—or for guilt?"
Guilt is leading the charge.

Alignment Audit:

Meaning: 4 – It no longer feels self-honoring.

Energy: 3 – You dread the process and feel shame when you skip it.

Sustainability: 2 – Injuries, exhaustion, and resentment are piling up.

Fulfillment Score: **3 / 10**

Interpretation: *It is time to reframe your why. Return to movement that feels good. Discipline without compassion becomes self-abandonment.*

The Sabbatical or Retreat

You have stepped away from the grind. There is quiet. There is clarity. You are not "producing"—but you are healing. And something within you is waking back up.

The Rich Life Filter:

"Am I honoring the space I longed for—or rushing to fill it again?"
You are finally listening.

Alignment Audit:

Meaning: 9 – Deep reconnection with your deeper self.

Energy: 8 – You are recharging and realigning.

Sustainability: 6 – Short-term for now, but it is revealing long-term truths.

Fulfillment Score: **7.7 / 10**

Interpretation: *This is sacred space. Use it not to escape, but to reimagine. Let what emerges here influence what comes next.*

Key Insight Across All Scenarios

Whether it is your work, your body, your relationships, or your roles; *alignment is always speaking.*

The question is: **are you listening?**

The Fulfillment Framework does not give you answers. It gives you **better questions**—and a way to answer them from the inside out.

Companion Worksheet: Map Your Fulfillment
A Personal Practice for Clarity, Alignment, and Choice

This worksheet is designed to help you apply the Fulfillment Framework to your own life. Whether you are facing a major decision, reevaluating a current path, or simply feeling off-center, this is your place to pause, reflect, and realign.

You can use this monthly, quarterly, or whenever you feel the need to check in. Print it. Journal it. Revisit it. The goal is not perfection—it is presence.

Step 1: The Rich Life Filter

Before you begin scoring, ask yourself:

- "Does this opportunity, commitment, or path serve the life I actually want—or just the one I have been performing?"

Take a moment to answer honestly, without judgment.

If your answer is unclear or uncomfortable, that is already valuable insight.

Step 2: The Alignment Audit

Choose one area of focus—something you are currently navigating or considering:

- A job or project
- A relationship
- A health or lifestyle goal
- A creative pursuit
- A major decision
- A recurring habit

(Insert your own) [ ]

Now, rate this area using the three core dimensions of fulfillment:

Category	Score (1-10)	Why You Gave this Score
Meaning		
Energy		
Sustainability		

Be as honest and specific as you can. The more detail you give yourself, the more actionable your insights will become.

Step 3: Fulfillment Score + Reflection

Add your scores together and divide by 3 to find your average Fulfillment Score:

(Meaning + Energy + Sustainability) ÷ 3 = [ ] **/ 10**

Now reflect:
- What is this telling me about my current alignment?
- Am I compromising one area to satisfy another?
- What might need to shift—externally or internally?
- Is this a season to **deepen, adjust, pause,** or **release?**

Step 4: Recalibration Practice

What do you want to do with this insight?

☐ *Keep going* – I am on track.

☐ *Recalibrate* – Something needs to shift.

☐ *Pause* – I need more time or clarity before deciding.

☐ *Let go* – This no longer aligns with who I am becoming.

You do not need a five-year plan. You just need your next step—one that honors your truth today.

Summary

This worksheet is not about judgment. It is about alignment.

Return to it often. Let it evolve with you, shifting as your life shifts and deepening as you grow. Let it remind you that you always have a choice—not just in what you do, but in how fully you live.

Reflection Prompts

Questions to Realign, Reground, and Recommit

Fulfillment does not come from doing more. It comes from *noticing more*—about what feels right, what feels off, and what wants to shift.

These prompts are not here to judge you. They are here to reveal the subtle signals you have been too busy to hear.

Use them as part of your Recalibration Practice.

As a journaling ritual.

As a check-in before major decisions—or in the quiet in-between moments of everyday life.

1. What area of my life feels most aligned right now?

Start with what is working.

- Where do you feel most at home in yourself?
- What activity, role, or relationship lights you up—not because of the result, but because of how it feels in the moment?

This is your North Star. Understand it. Protect it.

And if possible—expand it.

2. What am I doing that looks successful but feels off?

This is where the mask starts to slip.

- What are you carrying because it looks good from the outside—even if it feels empty inside?
- Where are you performing instead of choosing?

You do not have to quit immediately. But you do need to get curious. Because success without alignment is a slow form of erosion—and eventually, it shows.

3. Where am I compromising one part of the framework to satisfy another?

Sometimes, we hold on to something that feels meaningful—even if it is depleting.

Other times, we pursue something sustainable—but it lacks soul.

Check your balance.

- Are you trading Energy for Achievement? Sustainability for Applause? Meaning for Momentum?
- What would a more honest integration look like?

4. What small shift would increase my fulfillment this month?

You do not need an overhaul. You need a 5% shift in the direction of wholeness.

- Saying no to something that drains you.
- Saying yes to something you have postponed.
- Protecting your mornings.
- Reclaiming your evenings.
- Allowing stillness without guilt.

Big change begins with small honesty.

5. If I fully trusted myself, what would I do next?

This is the question underneath all the others.

If you were not afraid of disappointing others, missing out, or being misunderstood...

- What would you choose?
- What would you stop doing?
- What would you start?
- What would you return to?

The answer is already inside you. These prompts simply help you hear it.

Closing Thought

Fulfillment Is not a Destination. It is a Design Practice.

You do not find fulfillment by accident.

You do not stumble into it at the end of a checklist.

You create it—intentionally, repeatedly, and imperfectly—by the way you live, choose, and realign.

The Fulfillment Framework does not promise ease. It offers clarity. It gives you a way to listen when life gets noisy. A way to check your alignment before you lose yourself in momentum. A way to return to who you are, even when the world tells you to keep performing.

You now have the tools:

The Rich Life Filter – to cut through the noise.

The Alignment Audit – to assess what is true.

The Fulfillment Score – to reflect with honesty.

The Recalibration Practice – to evolve with grace.

This is not a one-time exercise. It is a rhythm. A compass. A way of walking through the world on your own terms. Because success without fulfillment is a quiet form of suffering.

But success *with* fulfillment? That is where the rich life begins.

Because not everything that counts can be counted. And not everything that is counted actually counts.

You do not have to run harder.

You do not have to chase louder.

You just must pause long enough to listen—and choose again.

Fulfillment is not the end of the road.

It is the way you walk it.

IV

Living the Curve

FROM KNOWING TO BECOMING

You have come a long way.

You have questioned the chase. You have
felt the subtle ache of misalignment and
named what the world rarely gives us space
to say aloud: that achievement without
meaning is never enough. You have paused.
You have listened. You have redefined
success, discovered your Satisfaction
Threshold, and returned to stillness.

But clarity alone does not transform us.

Embodiment does.

Part 4 is where the work becomes life.

- Not in grand gestures, but in quiet rhythms.
- Not in breakthroughs, but in presence.
- Not in knowing more, but in living what you already know.

This is the practice of integration.

To live the Fulfillment Curve is not to arrive at a perfect, peaceful destination. It is to walk forward with new eyes. It is to let alignment become a habit. Simplicity, a design choice. Joy, a measure. And wholeness—not something to earn—but something to return to.

In *Chapter 10*, we begin with a reorientation: what it truly means to live from the inside out. We examine how easy it is to perform a version of ourselves for the world—and how radical it is to reclaim our own voice. This is where alignment becomes a daily devotion, rooted not in rebellion but in return.

In *Chapter 11*, we clear the space. Not to do less for its own sake, but to release what never belonged. This is the chapter of simplification. Of subtraction. Of choosing fewer things more deeply—and learning that peace is not the absence of ambition, but the presence of clarity.

And in *Chapter 12*, we arrive—not at an ending, but at a beginning. A beginning where fulfillment is no longer something you seek, but something you choose. Intentionally. Repeatedly. With your energy, your time, your attention, your truth.

This is what it means to *live* the Fulfillment Curve.

- To let your inside become your compass.
- To let your peace lead your pace.
- To let your soul have a say.

Not as an ideal. But as your new normal.

This part of the journey is quiet, grounded, and unshakably yours.

Welcome to the rich life—not as a someday. But as a way.
Let's begin.

10

CHAPTER TEN

Stories, reflections, and tools
for aligning your external drive
with your internal compass.

Living from the Inside Out

*W*e spend so much of
life learning how to fit in—how
to succeed, how to be liked, how
to win the approval of others.
At some point, we begin to
mistake those external signals for
truth. Likes become validation.
Promotions become purpose.
Applause becomes identity.

But all of it is borrowed.
And what is borrowed
can be taken away.

Living from the outside in is like building a house on sand. The structure might look impressive, but it shifts with every storm. When expectations change or validation dries up, you are left unmoored—constantly adjusting, constantly performing, never quite arriving.

Living from the inside out is something else entirely.

It does not mean ignoring the world. It means choosing to meet the world from a place of alignment. It means letting your values shape your goals, not the other way around. It is about honoring what is true for you—even if it is inconvenient, unconventional, or misunderstood.

This chapter is an invitation to reorient. To stop measuring your life by how it looks… and start shaping it by how it feels.

To stop chasing applause… and start listening for resonance.

To stop outsourcing your worth… and start coming home to it.

Because fulfillment does not come from meeting other people's expectations. It comes from meeting your own truth with courage.

The Outside-In Default

Most of us do not choose to live from the outside in. We inherit it.

From an early age, we are taught to read the room before we read ourselves. We are praised for pleasing others. Rewarded for performance. Graded, measured, evaluated—until we begin to believe that our worth is something to be earned.

The world hands us a script:

- Be successful.
- Look the part.
- Climb the ladder.
- Stay busy.
- Be liked.
- Be better than.

And we follow it—not because we are shallow, but because we have been conditioned to believe this is the path to a good life. That if we just play the part well enough, we will eventually feel whole.

But something is off.

Because this outside-in life is built on reaction. We respond to what is expected of us. We perform for what is praised. We compare, adjust, strive—and somewhere along the way, we lose touch with what we actually want. What feels true. What matters deeply.

Psychologists call this "self-alienation" or "incongruence"—when our outer behavior no longer reflects our inner truth. Over time, this disconnect drains vitality and joy. But it can be reversed. Self-congruence, by contrast, is when our actions align with our identity and values—leading to emotional resilience, clarity, and deep satisfaction.

The result?

A life full of motion but lacking meaning. Success that does not satisfy. Achievements that feel strangely empty. A gnawing sense that we are doing everything "right" but still feel misaligned.

The outside-in default keeps us *performing* instead of *living*. It is not just exhausting—it is disorienting. Because no matter how fast we run or how much we acquire, we are always chasing a moving target. And the further we chase, the further we drift from ourselves.

This is where the curve begins to bend. Not because we failed. But because we finally stopped to ask:

Whose life am I living?

Signs You are Living Outside-In

When you are living outside-in, you often do not realize it—because from the outside, everything might look "fine." Or even impressive. You are achieving. You are admired. You are doing what people say they wish they could do.

But something is missing.

There is a subtle dissonance between your outer life and your inner truth. A quiet tension you cannot quite name. You may not even feel unhappy—but you feel unfulfilled. Like you are playing a role in a well-rehearsed script but forgetting who you were before the script began.

Here are some common signs you have been living from the outside in:

1. Chronic Comparison

You measure your progress by someone else's path. You scroll through other people's lives and feel either less than or behind. You chase goals not because they are meaningful to you, but because they are what people in your field *should* be doing. Your compass is not internal—it is reactive.

Self-check: *If social media disappeared tomorrow, would you still want what you are chasing?*

2. Decision Paralysis Based on Perception

You hesitate to make choices unless they are "optically correct." You worry more about how your decision *looks* than how it feels. You ask, "What will people think?" more than, "What do I want?" And you are exhausted from rehearsing the imaginary judgments of others before making a move.

Self-check: *Are you editing your life to stay likable?*

3. A Nagging Emptiness Despite External Success

On paper, you have done everything right. But it still does not feel like *you have arrived*. The celebration does not land. The recognition feels fleeting. You keep upping the stakes, hoping the next milestone will finally make you feel full. But the bar just keeps moving.

Self-check: *Have you achieved things you thought would fulfill you—but did not?*

4. Over Identification with Titles, Possessions, or Accolades

Your sense of self is tangled in what you *do*, *own*, or *achieve*. You find it hard to separate your worth from your resume. You cling to labels—CEO, parent, artist, overachiever—as a source of identity, not expression. Without them, you feel exposed.

Self-check: *Who are you when you are not performing, achieving, or being admired?*

5. Lack of Joy in the Journey

The process feels like a grind, not a calling. You are always rushing toward the next thing. Life becomes a checklist, not a creative act. You rarely pause to ask if the direction still aligns—because momentum has replaced intention.

Self-check: Are you chasing outcomes that no longer feel alive to you?

These signs are not failures. They are signals.

They are not here to shame you—they are here to *wake you.* To remind you that there is another way to live. One that honors your inner world as the source of your outer life.

What It Means to Live from the Inside Out

Living from the inside out is not about withdrawing from the world. It is about meeting it with your whole self—awake, aligned, and undivided.

It means your decisions are guided not by the volume of voices around you, but by the quiet conviction within you. It is not about abandoning ambition. It is about aligning it.

It is not about ignoring success, recognition, or achievement—but about no longer needing them to feel worthy or well.

This is not the easy path. But it is the real one.

Because inside-out living is not passive. It is not drifting. It is not a rejection of ambition or excellence. In fact, it requires more intention, more courage, and more clarity than the reactive path ever will. It asks you to show up with depth, not just drive. With truth, not just tactics.

Here is what begins to shift when you live this way:

Alignment over Approval

You stop making decisions to please the crowd.

Instead of asking, "Will this impress them?" you ask, "Is this true for me?" You no longer contort yourself to fit into rooms you have outgrown or roles that mute your voice. You let internal clarity—not applause—set the direction.

Approval is fleeting. **Alignment endures.**

Values over Validation

You let your core values guide how you spend your time, your energy, and your resources.

You move from auto-pilot to awareness, filtering your commitments through a lens of meaning. Does this nourish what I care about? Does this reflect who I am becoming?

Validation is reactive. **Values are rooted.**

Fulfillment over Performance

You stop living for the highlight reel. You prioritize what feels good on the inside—even if it looks unglamorous or unconventional from the outside. You recognize that performance without presence is hollow—and that true fulfillment comes not from being admired, but from being whole.

Performance seeks applause. **Fulfillment seeks resonance.**

Living from the inside out is an act of devotion. Not to ego—but to essence. Not to control—but to clarity.

It is choosing to build a life that does not just *look* good—but *feels* real.

It will not always make sense to others. But it will make sense to you.

And that is the beginning of freedom.

Living from the inside out is not about ignoring the world. It is about no longer letting it define you.

It means your decisions are guided not by the volume of voices around you, but by the quiet conviction within you. It is not about abandoning ambition. It is about aligning it.

When we live from the inside out, we are no longer chasing approval. We are expressing truth.

Studies show that people who experience high levels of self-congruence—the alignment between values, identity, and behavior—report greater psychological well-being, motivation, and energy. They have fewer regrets and clearer decision-making frameworks.

This is not rebellion. It is return. Return to your inner compass. Return to agency. Return to a life that feels like it belongs to you.

You may still reach for goals, grow a business, build a family, make bold moves—but you will do it from a grounded place. Not to prove. Not to impress. But to fulfill.

Living from the inside out is not a one-time decision. It is a daily practice of listening inward and responding outward—in that order.

The Three Practices of Inside-Out Living

Living from within does not happen by accident. It is a practice—a way of being that must be chosen, cultivated, and protected.

After years (or decades) of living by default—chasing approval, performing for praise, or checking the next external box—it takes intention to rewire the way you move through the world.

This is not about abandoning goals or retreating into solitude. It is about bringing your soul to the surface. Showing up aligned. And making daily decisions that reflect who you are—not just what others expect.

Here are three essential practices that support this shift:

1. Inner Listening

The world is loud. Your clarity will not be.

Inside-out living begins with the discipline of tuning in to the quiet voice of your own knowing. Not the voice of fear. Not the voice of ego. Not the voice of conditioning. But the steady, grounded voice beneath the noise.

This is where your compass lives. And to hear it, you must get still.

How to Practice:

- Begin each day with a pause—before the inbox, before the scroll.
- Ask simple questions: *What do I need today? What matters most right now?*
- Use journaling, meditation, or even silence in the shower as tools to check in.

The more often you return to yourself, the more quickly you will recognize when you have drifted.

2. Aligned Action

Clarity means nothing without movement.

Once you hear what is true, you have to live like you believe it. That is where courage comes in—because acting on your inner truth might mean saying no to what looks "right." Or stepping into something uncertain, unapproved, or unfamiliar.

But alignment does not demand perfection. It demands integrity.

How to Practice:

- Make decisions based on values, not optics.
- Do not just set goals—ask *why* they matter.
- Say yes only when your whole self is in agreement.
- Say no with kindness, but also with finality.

Each aligned action is a vote for the life you are meant to live—not just the one you have inherited.

3. Soulful Boundaries

You cannot live from the inside out if you are constantly pulled outside yourself.

Boundaries are not walls—they are clarity. They protect your energy. Your peace. Your priorities. And they remind you (and others) that your life is not a public playground—it is a sacred place.

Soulful boundaries are less about what you keep out, and more about what you choose to preserve.

How to Practice:

- Say no without explanation.
- Guard your attention—it is your most limited resource.

- Unsubscribe from what does not resonate: relationships, roles, even routines.
- Let people misunderstand you if that is the cost of staying true.

Protect the life you are building—even if others do not understand it. Especially then.

These three practices are not one-time resolutions. They are daily choices. They form the foundation of a life that is not *performed*, but *embodied*.

The more you live from the inside out, the less you will need to prove anything.

You will stop seeking applause because you are already standing in your truth.

Common Fears & Resistance

Letting go of the outside-in life can feel like freedom. But first, it feels like fear.

Even when we know we are out of alignment, even when we are exhausted from performing or quietly aching for something real, the shift to inside-out living can feel terrifying.

Why?

Because it threatens the very identity we have built.

We have spent years—sometimes our whole lives—perfecting the role we were told to play. The achiever. The provider. The high performer. The caretaker. The one who *has it all together*.

Living from within asks you to question that script. And anytime you question the script, the fear voice gets loud.

Here are some of the most common fears and forms of resistance that surface when you begin to make the shift:

"What if people do not understand?"

They might not.

Not everyone will clap for your clarity. Especially if your truth challenges the status quo, or their perception of you.

When you live from the inside out, you stop editing yourself for approval. That can feel disruptive to others—especially those who benefitted from your old compliance.

But here is the thing: if your alignment costs you someone else's comfort, it is still worth it.

Let go of being understood. Reach for being whole.

"What if I lose what I have built?"

Maybe you will.

Some relationships, roles, and routines were constructed to serve a version of you that no longer exists. Releasing them might feel like failure—but it is actually fidelity. To your growth. To your truth.

What is meant for the *real* you will remain. Or it will return in new form.

Shedding the false is not a loss. It is a homecoming.

"What if I disappoint people?"

You probably will.

Especially if you have been the dependable one. The agreeable one. The one who always says yes.

But disappointment is often the price of authenticity. And if you have been disappointing yourself to avoid disappointing others it is time to flip that equation.

You can disappoint others and still be a good person. But disappointing yourself over and over—that leaves a deeper scar.

"What if I do not know what I want?"

That is okay.

Most of us do not—at least not at first. When you have spent years chasing external markers, your inner voice can grow faint. But it is never gone. And the more you slow down, listen, and choose based on resonance instead of reaction, the clearer it becomes.

Clarity is not a lightning bolt. It is a signal you strengthen over time.

You do not have to know everything to begin. You just have to know what is no longer true—and trust that truth will rise in the quiet that follows.

Resistance is not weakness. It is a sign that you are nearing something sacred. Something real.

Let the fear be there. Let the doubts speak. But do not let them drive.

This shift is not easy.

But neither is living a life that looks good and feels wrong.

Stories from the Curve

The most powerful stories are not the ones where everything went right. They are the ones where someone stopped pretending—and started living.

The Executive Who Could Not Breathe

Jason had spent twenty years climbing. Ivy League education. Corner office. A seven-figure exit. On paper, he had it all. But something strange happened after the deal closed. He felt… empty. Not depressed. Not broken. Just hollow.

He tried filling the void with a new venture, but his energy never returned. Eventually, after months of restless pacing and tight-chested mornings, he canceled everything. Took a sabbatical. Traveled alone. Wrote every morning without knowing why.

It took him a year to realize he did not want to build another company. He wanted to build a life.

Today, Jason leads silent retreats for entrepreneurs. He still talks strategy—but with an entirely different metric of success: peace.

He stopped chasing impact and started embodying it.

The Teacher Who Had not Taught Herself

Elena loved her students. She had a gift for connection, for explaining big ideas with warmth. But over time, she found herself shrinking. The curriculum was rigid. The schedule unforgiving. She felt more like a manager than a mentor.

She had always dreamed of writing, but there was never time. One day, she gave herself a challenge: wake up 30 minutes early and write, just for herself. No goal. No judgment. Just truth.

A year later, those early morning fragments became a memoir. Then a speaking invitation. Then a new career—not in opposition to her teaching, but as its deeper expression.

She had not abandoned her role. She had expanded her life.

She gave herself permission to evolve.

The Builder Who Was Building the Wrong Thing

Marco was proud of the homes he built—strong, beautiful, admired. But over time, he felt like something was missing. Not from the structures, but from the process. He knew how to win bids. He knew how to please clients. But he was tired of cutting corners, of optimizing for aesthetics instead of meaning.

He began asking new questions: *What would I build if I was not trying to impress anyone? What if I created something that aligned with my values, not just the market?*

That shift gave birth to a new company. Fewer projects. Slower pace. Higher standards. Not just better homes—but a better way of working.

He realized the real project was himself.

These stories remind us that the curve does not flatten when you reach a milestone. It begins to rise when you begin to *listen.*

Not to the noise—but to the knowing.

Reflection Prompts: Your Inside-Out Inventory

Clarity begins with noticing. Before we can change how we live, we have to see how we are living now.

This inventory is not about judgment—it is about honesty.

It is a mirror, not a scoreboard. A way to check in, realign, and come home to what is true.

Set aside 15–20 minutes. Get quiet. Get still. And answer these prompts from a place of curiosity, not criticism.

Part 1: Awareness Check — Am I Living Outside-In?

Answer each statement with:

Always / Often / Sometimes / Rarely / Never

- I worry what others will think before
  I make important decisions.
- I feel pressure to maintain an image that
  does not fully match who I am.
- I achieve goals but often feel underwhelmed once I reach them.
- I compare myself to others and feel behind or inadequate.
- I say yes to things out of obligation, not desire.
- I feel anxious when I am not being productive or "useful."
- I find it hard to separate who I am from what I do.
- I delay joy, rest, or creativity until after I have "earned" it.

If you answered "Often" or "Always" to more than half of these, it may be time to recalibrate. Not because you are failing—because you are ready to live more freely.

Part 2: Alignment Scan — What is True for Me?

Write freely. Let it be messy. Let it be real.

- What parts of my life feel out of alignment right now?
  (Where do I feel drained, disoriented, or performative?)

- Where do I already live from the inside out?
  (Moments when I feel whole, grounded, or quietly proud.)

- What am I afraid might happen if I truly followed what I know is right for me?
  (Be honest—fear loses power when named.)

- What values do I want to center more deeply in my decisions?
  (List 3–5 core values you want to live by—not just believe in.)

- What would shift in my life if I honored those values more consistently?
  (Think habits, relationships, work, or how you speak to yourself.)

Part 3: A Small Reorientation

Now choose one small act of alignment. Not a grand gesture. A next step. Maybe it is a boundary you have been avoiding. Maybe it is a project that has been quietly calling your name. Maybe it is resting—even when no one gives you permission.

- What is one way I can live more inside-out this week?

Write it down. Then do it. Not because you have to—but because you are free to.

Closing Thought

The most radical thing you can do in a world of noise is to trust your own voice.

Living from the inside out is not a single decision. It is a thousand daily ones. It is the choice to pause before performing. To listen before leaping. To check in before you check out.

It is not always glamorous. It will not always be applauded.

But it will be *real*.

And that is what this chapter—and this curve—is all about.

Every time you choose your truth over someone else's script, you bend the curve toward fulfillment.

You were never meant to live as a reflection of someone else's expectations. You were meant to live as the clearest expression of who you are.

This is not rebellion. It is return.

Not the rejection of the world—but your reentry into it, with integrity.

Your path may look different from the one you started on.

That is okay. That is wisdom. Because fulfillment does not ask, *"How do I look while doing this?"* It asks, *"Am I home in myself while doing this?"*

And when the answer is yes—the outside can finally quiet down.

Because the inside has come alive.

CHAPTER ELEVEN

When Less is More

We live in a culture
that glorifies more.

More goals. More content. More
commitments. More tabs open—on
our screens and in our minds.

As if adding more is the
key to feeling whole.

As if productivity is proof of purpose.

But more does not
always mean better.

Sometimes more is just noise.

Somewhere along the way, we stopped asking where all this "more" is actually leading us.

We mistake volume for value.

We chase complexity, believing it reflects ambition.

But in the rush to keep up, we dilute the very thing we are after: meaning.

The irony is sharp. We are doing more than ever. And feeling more disconnected, more distracted, more depleted.

This chapter is an invitation to shift. Not to abandon ambition, but to refine it. Not to settle for less, but to choose less—intentionally.

Because fulfillment does not come from doing everything. It comes from doing the right things—deeply, and with presence.

Cognitive science backs this, too. Our brains are designed to process a finite amount of information. Excess input leads to decision fatigue, decreased focus, and chronic stress. Simplification is not just aesthetic. It is neurological.

This is the quiet power of subtraction.

Not as deprivation, but as clarity.

Not to shrink your life, but to shape it around what matters most.

When less is chosen with care, it does not leave you with emptiness. It leaves you with space.

- To breathe.
- To focus.
- To come home to yourself.

Welcome to the part of the journey where you do not add more to your life.

You uncover what is always been waiting underneath.

The Power of Subtraction

Subtraction is often misunderstood. We think it means shrinking. Withdrawing. Giving up.

But real subtraction is an act of refinement. A reclaiming of clarity. It is saying:

- I am no longer willing to chase what does not matter.
- I do not need to fill every inch of space to feel full.
- I trust that what remains is enough to build something rich.

Minimalism is not about deprivation. It is about discernment.

Psychologists call this "attentional alignment"—the practice of choosing where your energy goes, and letting go of the rest. And studies show that intentional simplification is linked to higher life satisfaction, reduced anxiety, and greater emotional availability.

In a world that glorifies accumulation, choosing less becomes a revolutionary act.

Simplicity as a Strategy for Depth

We often equate simplicity with lack. But in truth, it is a strategy for depth.

When you simplify, you create space:

- For your attention to land.
- For your nervous system to reset.
- For your relationships to feel you more fully.
- For your creativity to breathe.

Simplicity creates what some psychologists call "mental-white space"—a necessary condition for reflection, focus, and meaningful output.

What looks like quiet on the outside often signals alignment on the inside.

Simplifying is not about doing less for its own sake. It is about reducing friction so that what matters most can rise.

The 3 Domains of Simplification

Mental: Declutter your inner world. Let go of the narratives, loops, and obligations that do not belong to this version of you.

Physical: Edit your environment. Your surroundings either drain or support your clarity.

Emotional: Release roles, relationships, or expectations that no longer serve your peace.

Simplicity is not absence. It is presence with less noise.

Drowning in the Noise

We live in a world of too much.

- Too many tabs open—on our screens and in our minds.
- Too many commitments, goals, notifications, expectations.
- Too many voices telling us what we should want.

And somehow, we have come to accept this as normal. Not just normal—*necessary.* As if the volume of our activity is the measure of our worth. As if being stretched thin proves we are doing something right.

But beneath the productivity hacks and calendar color codes, a quiet truth lingers. We are overwhelmed—not just by what is required, but by what we have quietly agreed to take on. And every yes that is not aligned is a no to something that could have been.

The result? We lose track of what really matters.

- We mistake more for meaning.
- We confuse busy with important.
- We treat motion like progress—and forget to ask where we are actually going.

This is not just about time management. It is about energy—how we spend it, protect it, and restore it. It is about presence—our ability to show up for what matters, undistracted and whole. It is about fulfillment—because we cannot feel aligned when we are constantly overwhelmed.

It is about reclaiming the right to live *deliberately*—not reactively.

Because here is the truth: Fulfillment does not come from adding more—it comes from choosing less, with intention.

- Not less as in deprivation.
- Less as in *discernment.*
- Less as in finally having the space to listen—to your needs, your values, your inner compass.

Simplicity, when chosen, is not lack. It is clarity. It is the quiet power of knowing what to keep—and the courage to release what you never needed.

It is a return.

- To what matters.
- To what endures.
- To the life that fits—not the one that exhausts.

The Clarity of Subtraction

There is a hidden power in subtraction.

Not the kind that diminishes—but the kind that reveals.

We are taught to measure growth by what we *add*: more tasks, more goals, more accomplishments. But often, clarity arrives not through addition—but through removal. Removing the clutter reveals what matters. Saying no strengthens the power of your yes. Clearing space creates capacity—not just for doing, but for being.

Subtraction is how we carve meaning from chaos. It is how we hear the signal beneath the noise.

Because less is not lack.
Less is **leverage.**
It is focus. Precision. Freedom.

When you stop trying to be everything to everyone, you finally become someone to yourself.

And when you focus on fewer things that truly matter, your impact—and your peace—*expand*. Not because you are doing more, but because you are finally aligned.

Subtraction is not the enemy of ambition. It is how ambition becomes sustainable. It is how we trade frantic movement for meaningful momentum.

This is the shift. From scattered energy to centered intention. From chasing everything to choosing what matters most. From "How much can I handle?" to "What is truly worth holding?"

The Fulfillment Funnel

(visual breakdown)

Funnel Level	Description
Top: **Overload Zone**	Where life gets crowded with too many inputs—emails, meetings, commitments, and the endless stream of demands that leave you scattered and reactive.
Middle: **Subtraction Layer**	The intentional pause: filtering out what doesn't serve you by saying no, simplifying routines, and reclaiming focus. This is where boundaries start reshaping your day.
Bottom: **Clarity Core**	The distilled essence: what's left after subtraction. Clear priorities, values, and aligned actions that generate fulfillment and a sense of meaning.

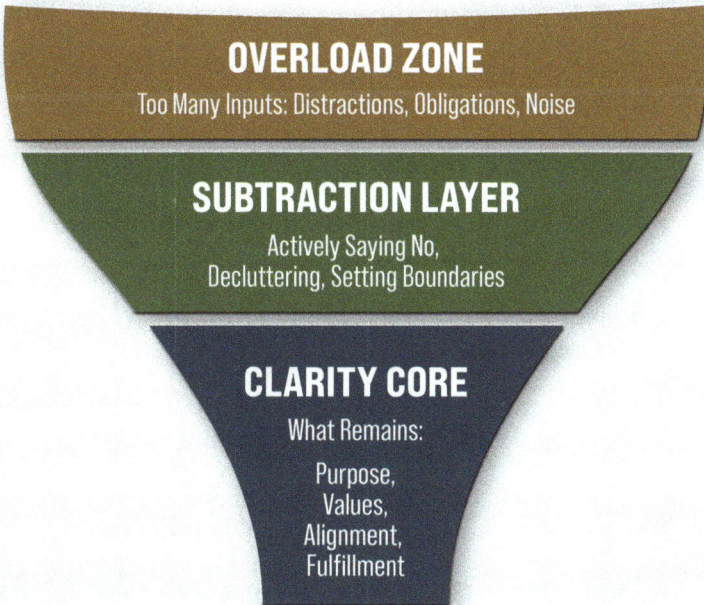

OVERLOAD ZONE
Too Many Inputs: Distractions, Obligations, Noise

SUBTRACTION LAYER
Actively Saying No,
Decluttering, Setting Boundaries

CLARITY CORE
What Remains:

Purpose,
Values,
Alignment,
Fulfillment

As we remove what does not align, we create space for what truly fulfills us. Fulfillment is not a result of more—but of choosing less, more wisely.

The 3 Domains of Simplification

Simplifying your life does not mean shrinking it—it means *clarifying* it. It means removing the unnecessary, so the essential can finally breathe. Fulfillment is not found in how much we juggle, but in how fully we show up for what matters.

To do that, we must simplify across three key domains: **mental**, **emotional**, and **physical**. Each layer influences the others. When one becomes cluttered, the rest follow. But when we clear space in one, we often find clarity in all.

1. Mental Simplicity – *Declutter Your Inner World*

- Your mind is not meant to be a storage unit—it is meant to be *a space of presence, insight, and creativity.* But in a culture of constant input, we often crowd it with noise: indecision, comparison, rumination.

- Mental simplicity means creating space to think clearly and live intentionally.

- Stop overthinking every decision—*not everything deserves your mental bandwidth.*

- Build in quiet rituals: stillness, journaling, meditation. These are not luxuries. They are lifelines to clarity.

- Let go of outdated narratives. The story that served you five years ago may now be the story holding you back.

- Mental simplicity does not empty your mind—it *unclutters* it, so you can actually hear your own wisdom.

2. Emotional Simplicity – *Stop Carrying What Is not Yours*

- We often mistake empathy for obligation, and kindness for self-erasure. But carrying the emotional weight of others—or of the past—comes at the cost of your own peace.

- Emotional simplicity is not cold or detached. It is discerning.

- Drop the need to please everyone. You are not responsible for managing others' expectations.

- Release the past through forgiveness—not as a favor to others, but as a gift to your own nervous system.

- Set emotional boundaries, not to push others away, but to keep your own center intact.

- When your emotions are clear and self-owned, you do not just feel lighter—you become more grounded, more available, more you.

3. Physical Simplicity – *Let Your Environment Reflect Your Values*

- Our external world either supports or sabotages our inner clarity. If your space, schedule, or stuff is chaotic, your energy will be too.

- Physical simplicity is not about aesthetic minimalism—it is about functional alignment.

- Clear your calendar of obligations that drain more than they give. Make room for what restores you.

- Design your spaces to reduce friction and increase focus. Let your environment become a quiet ally.

- Choose quality over quantity—not just in what you buy, but in what you pursue. Depth is more fulfilling than breadth.

- When your physical world aligns with your values, it becomes easier to live in alignment everywhere else.

A Final Insight

Simplification is not subtraction for its own sake. It is a practice of purposeful refinement. Not to do less—but to live more fully.

Because the fewer things you chase, the more space you have to *be here*. And that is where fulfillment begins.

A Life That Breathes

When you simplify, something beautiful happens.

You begin to feel spacious again.

You have room: for joy to arise unplanned; for rest to happen without guilt; for conversations to stretch beyond efficiency. You regain *margin*—that sacred space between obligation and exhaustion where creativity, presence, and connection can flourish.

You **reclaim time**—not just on your calendar, but **in your soul.**

This is how life begins to breathe again. Not just in the physical sense—but in the spiritual, emotional, and existential sense.

You inhale peace—because there is finally space for it to land.

You exhale pressure—because you are no longer carrying what was never meant to be yours.

A simplified life is not a smaller life.

It is a more *alive* life.

- One with room to move, to feel, to change.
- One where the pace aligns with your values.
- One where fulfillment is not squeezed between the cracks, but *woven into the rhythm* of your days.

Because when your life breathes, so do you.

Questions for Simplicity

Simplicity begins with awareness. Before you can subtract, you must *see*—clearly, honestly—what is taking up space. These questions are not about productivity. They are about alignment. About returning to a life that reflects your values, not just your obligations.

Take your time with each one. Let them open space within you.

1. What am I doing out of habit, not intention?

We often stay busy with routines that no longer serve us. Rituals inherited from a former self or borrowed from someone else's definition of success.

Ask: Does this action reflect who I am now—or who I used to be?

Simplicity starts when habit gives way to choice.

2. What would I drop if I stopped trying to impress anyone?

So much of our complexity is performative—designed to maintain an image, gain approval, or avoid judgment.

But if you were free from the gaze of others, what would you release?

Ask: What would remain if I only lived for meaning, not applause?

3. What 3 things bring the most peace in my life?

Fulfillment often hides in plain sight—in the small, grounding rituals and quiet moments we overlook.

Make a list. Protect those things.

Ask: How can I give these more space, more time, more reverence?

4. What 3 things bring the most noise?

Noise is not always loud. Sometimes it shows up as mental clutter, emotional drain, or constant interruption.

These are the hidden thieves of your clarity.

Ask: What boundaries—or goodbyes—do I need to consider?

A Gentle Prompt

Do not rush to fix or rearrange. Start by noticing.

Simplicity is not a purge— it is a **recalibration.**

The goal is not less for the sake of it. It is less of what does not matter, so you can make space for what deeply does.

The Courage to Let Go

Letting go is not always easy.

Even when we know something no longer serves us, we hesitate.

Not because we love the thing itself, but because of what it *represents*:

our sense of worth; our role in others' lives; our identity as someone who handles it all.

You may grieve the identity attached to being busy, involved, productive. After all, these roles often brought praise. They gave you a place, a rhythm, a narrative. But were they ever truly *yours*?

This is the quiet crossroads of simplification. The place where, or moment when, you begin to choose presence over performance. Peace over proving. Clarity over complexity.

And that choice takes courage.

It is not just about what you release. It is about who you are willing to become when you do.

Letting go is an act of trust.

- Trust that you will still be enough without the extras.
- Trust that your worth is not found in your busyness, but in your being.
- Trust that by saying no, you are actually saying *yes* to something deeper.

You are not here to be everything to everyone. You are here to live in a way that feels honest.

- Quietly aligned.
- Deeply rooted.
- Truly free.

And sometimes, the most courageous thing you can do is simply... **stop**. Not because you have given up but because you have finally come home.

A Life That Breathes

Take a quiet moment.

Close your eyes. Let your body soften.
Let your breath return to its natural rhythm—unforced, unhurried.

Feel the space you have just created—not just in your mind, but in your spirit.

Now imagine your life… simplified. Not emptied, but refined.
Not less in meaning—but less in noise.

Notice what remains:

**The relationships that nourish you. The work that energizes you.
The quiet joys that remind you who you are.**

Let go—gently—of everything else.

Breathe in: clarity.
Breathe out: pressure.
Breathe in: alignment.
Breathe out: expectation.

You are not falling behind. You are coming back to yourself.

Affirmation

I release what no longer serves me.
I honor what brings me peace.
I trust that less can be more—when less is chosen with love.
I do not need to prove anything. I only need to live what is true.

Reflection Prompts: Letting Go, Lightening Up

Simplicity does not begin with what you toss into a donation box. It begins with a moment of honesty. Of noticing what you have been carrying—and asking whether you still need to.

These prompts are not just questions.

They are invitations.

- To pause.
- To feel.
- To choose again.

1. What am I holding onto that is weighing me down?

It could be a commitment.

A belief.

A relationship.

An identity that once felt necessary—but now just feels heavy.

Ask: Why am I still holding this? Who would I be without it?

Letting go is not weakness.

It is *wisdom.*

2. Where am I complicating what could be simple?

Sometimes complexity feels safer—like a buffer between us and the vulnerability of being seen. But often, it is just a distraction in disguise.

Ask: Am I adding steps, stories, or expectations that do not need to be there?

Simplicity is not laziness.

It is *liberation.*

3. What one thing could I release this week to feel lighter?

You do not have to overhaul everything. Fulfillment begins with small, honest edits.

Choose one thing.

Something you have outgrown.

Something that no longer aligns.

And give yourself permission to let it go.

Then notice: How does your body feel afterward? Your mind? Your breath?

Lightness is not the absence of responsibility.

It is the presence of *clarity.*

Closing Thought

You do not need to do more. You need to do *less.*

Less of what distracts, drains, or disconnects you from what truly matters. And *more* of what brings you home to yourself.

The goal was never to be everything to everyone. The goal is to be whole. Present. Rooted in what is real.

Fulfillment does not live in the margins of your to-do list. It does not wait for the next achievement, the next addition, the next "one more thing."

In the end, it is not the extras that give life meaning. It is the essentials—the few things that make you feel alive, aligned, and at peace.

So let the noise fall away.

Let the clutter lose its grip.

And return—gently, intentionally—to what is simple, honest, and *true*.

Because that is where fulfillment lives.

Not in the excess.

But in the essence.

Simplifying is not stepping back. It is stepping in.

Not to abandon your ambition. But to clarify its roots.

Because when you subtract what does not serve, you are left with the essence of what does.

And that essence is enough.

12

CHAPTER TWELVE

A final meditation on what it
means to choose fulfillment
intentionally—and repeatedly.

Choosing a Rich Life

ARRIVAL WAS NEVER A PLACE

You have made it to the end of this book. But what if the real destination… is you?

Not the version of you that is always striving. Not the one chasing the next milestone or managing expectations. But the version rooted in presence.

Whole, aware, and awake.

We are taught to see fulfillment as something we *reach*.

A finish line. A title. A moment when the noise finally stops.

But what if arrival is not a place at all? What if it is a *choice*? A choice to live fully *here*, before everything is figured out?

Because the truth is: life will always be unfinished. There will always be more to do, more to become, more to fix. But that does not mean you have to wait to feel whole.

We are taught that **fulfillment** lives somewhere on the other side of **achievement**.

Once we hit the milestone, land the role, reach the number—then we can feel peace. Then we can rest. Then we can finally exhale.

But that kind of arrival never quite arrives.

Because peace is not a finish line.

It is a choice.

The richest lives are not built by those who never get lost. They are built by those who learn to return.

- To return to alignment.
- To return to intention.
- To return to what matters most.

Narrative identity theory teaches us that meaning comes when we see ourselves as the authors of our lives. Not passive characters or reactive victims—but creative agents. People who shape the arc of their becoming.

I Am Already Home

Your Affirmation of Peace

I no longer chase wholeness—I return to it.

I release the need to prove, to earn,
to outrun my own enoughness.

I honor the life that is here,
not the one I have been taught to wait for.

I choose presence over perfection.

Peace over pressure.

Alignment over achievement.

The rich life is not out there.

It lives in me—when I choose to live with
intention, clarity, and truth.

I am not behind.

I am not incomplete.

I AM ALREADY HOME

Choosing a rich life is about authorship.

And authorship is about awareness.

The rich life begins when you stop postponing your peace. When you stop outsourcing your worth to outcomes. When you stop measuring your life by what is missing—and start living from what is already true.

This is not about giving up on growth. It is about choosing to grow from a place of alignment, not lack.

It is the shift from chasing to becoming.

From proving to belonging.

From running toward something to *realizing you are already standing in it.*

The **richest life**
is not the one
with the most trophies—
it is the one
with the **most truth.**

The quiet confidence of someone who knows who they are and chooses to live accordingly. Even when the world says to keep climbing, keep accumulating, keep comparing.

So yes—you have reached the end.

But maybe, just maybe, what you have really reached…

Is the beginning of something deeper.

The beginning of your own arrival.

What it Means to Choose

Choosing is active. It is not something that happens to you— it is something you *claim*. It is not default. It is not drift. It is intention, embodied.

To choose is to wake up to your own agency. To stop waiting for permission. To stop postponing your peace until everything is perfect.

Choosing is sacred—because it reclaims what is yours to direct:

- Your energy.
- Your attention.
- Your one, unrepeatable life.

To choose a rich life means:

You no longer outsource your definition of success. You decide what matters—based on your values, not external applause.

You no longer chase validation. You build a life of integrity, where worth is measured from the inside out.

You say no with strength. Not out of rejection, but out of reverence—for your time, your truth, your direction.

- You say yes with soul.
- Yes to what restores you.
- Yes to what aligns.
- Yes to what brings you alive.

And most of all: You live each day as if your peace, your joy, and your alignment matter.

Because they do.

They always have.

You do not choose the rich life once. You choose it every day.

- In small decisions.
- In the boundaries you hold.
- In the energy you protect.
- In the values you return to when the world goes loud.

You choose it over and over.

- In the quiet moments.
- In the small decisions.
- In the way you treat your time, your body, your gifts.

Choosing is not a one-time declaration. It is a daily devotion.

- To living on purpose.
- To living awake.
- To living true.

Choosing is Sacred

There is something holy about reclaiming your power of choice. Not to control everything—but to live with clarity in the midst of uncertainty.

Because life will always ask for more.

More goals. More output. More proof.

But fulfillment asks something different.

- It asks you to listen.
- It asks you to trust.
- It asks you to choose—even when the world around you does not understand the choice.

Choosing is not about getting it perfect.

It is about getting it honest.

The Fulfillment Curve in Motion

If you look back, the curve you have traveled is not a straight line. It bends. It loops. It repeats.

But every bend brought wisdom.

Every loop offered a lesson.

And now, your life has rhythm.

Now, you have a framework.

Now, you can return.

Not to some old version of yourself—but to the deeper self you have been building all along.

Because this is the gift of alignment:

- Not a life without friction.
- But a life where the friction has purpose.

You now understand the arc. Not just as an idea, but as a lived experience.

Part I: The Chase

Where we begin, driven by ambition, addicted to achievement, and unaware of the deeper cost. We run hard, fueled by the belief that success will eventually lead to satisfaction. We measure ourselves by external milestones, unaware that the finish line keeps moving.

Part II: The Awakening

Where something cracks open. Where we realize that achievement without alignment leaves us empty. This is where discomfort becomes clarity, and the questions begin to change. We start to ask not just *what am I doing?* but *why am I doing it?*

Part III: The Integration

Where we rebuild from the inside out. Where success and soul begin to coexist. We no longer abandon parts of ourselves in pursuit of progress. Instead, we design a life where growth is rooted in values, and goals serve meaning—not ego.

Part IV: The Embodiment

Where fulfillment becomes lived. Not a concept, not a chapter, but a rhythm. This is where we let go of what no longer serves. Where simplicity becomes strength, and peace becomes a compass. Where we do not just know our truth—we live it.

But here is the truth.

This curve is not linear. It does not ask you to "arrive" and stay put. It is cyclical.

A spiral of evolution and return.

You will revisit the chase. You will forget, drift, get caught up. But now, you have the tools to notice the drift sooner—and return faster.

You will awaken again—deeper this time. Because each loop through the curve invites more honesty, more wholeness, more grace.

And each time you integrate, you will live with more intention, more clarity, more ease. You will embody fulfillment not as an outcome—but as a way of being.

That is what it means to live the Fulfillment Curve in motion. Not as a path to complete, but as a practice to return to. A rhythm that supports you, grounds you, and reminds you.

You do not have to chase what you can choose.

You do not have to prove what you can live.

You do not have to wait for someday— When the richness of life is already here.

Before You Choose: Listening at All Levels

Introducing The Soul Scale™

You have explored the arc. You have seen the shift from chasing to choosing, from proving to becoming. And now you stand at the threshold of something deeper. Not just the awareness of what matters—but the practice of living it.

But here is the challenge: We are multi-layered beings. We think. We feel. We know—often all at once, and not always in agreement.

Sometimes your *head* will say one thing. Your *heart* will whisper another. And your *soul*—quietly, patiently—will point you toward something deeper still.

That is where the *Soul Scale™* comes in.

This simple tool invites you to pause before you choose. To check in across three distinct dimensions of inner wisdom:

1. Head (Logic)

Does this make sense? Is this choice clear, coherent, and aligned with what I know intellectually or practically?

2. Heart (Desire)

Do I want this? Does it stir joy, passion, or longing? Is there energy and emotional pull?

3. Soul (Truth)

Does this feel right—even if it is hard? Does it resonate at a deeper level—beyond logic, beyond preference? Would I still choose it if no one else ever knew?

You do not need all three to scream "yes." But when one feels off, the Soul Scale helps you notice. It helps you pause. It invites honesty.

And when all three align—you will feel it. Not as excitement. Not even as clarity. But as peace. Quiet. Inner congruence.

This is not a test. It is a practice of alignment. A way of making decisions that honor the full spectrum of who you are.

Because true fulfillment is not found in outcomes alone. It is found in the integrity of your inner life.

When your thoughts, your desires, and your deepest truth walk together in the same direction.

So before you step forward, before you say yes or no, before you redefine success or recalibrate your life—take a moment.

Check in.

Not just with your calendar. But with your head. With your heart. With your soul.

And then, from that place of clarity—

Choose.

The Invitation: Live Aligned

You have done the inner work.

You have reflected, released, remembered.

Now comes the invitation. Not to master anything. Not to rush into something new. But to *live* what you already know.

Let this be your new rhythm.

Not a set of rules, but a return. Not a rigid formula, but a living compass that brings you back—again and again—to what matters.

Clarity before action.

So you are not just moving—you are moving with direction.

Let your "yes" be rooted in truth, not urgency. Let your "no" be a boundary, not a burden.

Meaning before milestones.

Because goals without soul are hollow.

Let your definitions of success reflect who you are—not who you think you should be.

Joy in the process, not just the outcome.

Because this life is not a checklist.

It is a journey of becoming.

And fulfillment lives in the middle, not at the end.

Use the tools.

Not as quick fixes, but as rituals of remembering.

Filter your decisions through the Rich Life Filter™

Ask: Does this align with my values, vision, and vitality?

Let it strip away the noise and surface-level distractions, revealing what truly supports your richest life.

Evaluate with the Alignment Audit

Ask: Is this meaningful? Energizing? Sustainable?

Do not score for performance—score for truth. Let this lens sharpen your awareness and clarify your path.

Re-center with the Fulfillment Score

Life will drift. That is natural. This score brings you back—not to perfection, but to alignment. It reminds you that fulfillment is not a finish line—it is a relationship.

Tune in with the Soul Scale™

Because sometimes logic is loud, but your soul already knows. Head. Heart. Soul. When they align, so do you.

These tools are not checkboxes.
They are practices.
They are Guides.
They are gentle mirrors that reflect you back to yourself.

You do not need to earn your way to a rich life. You only need to choose it—deliberately, consistently, lovingly.

- Live aligned.
- Live awake.
- Live true.

Because when you do, fulfillment stops being something you chase. And becomes the way you move through everything.

This Is Your Rich Life

This is not about reinventing your life overnight.

It is about *reclaiming* it—one honest, intentional choice at a time.

- You have done the work.
- You have questioned what you were chasing.
- You have remembered what matters.
- You have begun to align your actions with your truth.

And now, the invitation is simple—though not always easy.

- **Live like it matters.**
- Not to everyone.
- Not for applause.
- But for you.

Because your richest life will not always be loud. It may not look extraordinary from the outside. It may not always make sense to others.

But it will be **yours**—and that is what makes it rich.

A life where your goals serve your soul.
Where achievement is rooted in meaning, not validation.

A life where you grow without grinding.
Where effort is sacred—but not sacrificial.
Where you honor your energy, your rhythm, your season.

A life where fulfillment is not some distant mountaintop—
but the ground beneath your feet.
Steady. Quiet. Enough.

You do not have to chase it. You do not have to earn it. You simply have to choose it—again and again. Because the rich life was never out there. It is been waiting here all along.

Final Reflection

A rich life is not something you chase. It is something you choose. Not once. But again and again.

- With your presence.
- With your priorities.
- With your peace.

This is the fulfillment curve in motion:

- Less about arrival.
- More about return.
- Less about the next thing.
- More about this thing.

This moment. This breath. This step.
You are not behind. You are not late.
You are home. And from here, anything is possible.

Closing Thought: A Final Blessing

May you no longer measure your life by how much you do—
but by how fully you live.

May you have the courage to stop performing,
the clarity to stop proving,
and the peace to stop chasing.

May you trust the wisdom already within you—
the voice that knows when to push,
and when to pause.
When to reach,
and when to rest.

May your goals serve your soul.
May your path feel like home.
And may you return—again and again—
to what is simple,
what is honest,
what is true.

This is not the end.
It is the beginning of a new rhythm.
A life lived not from pressure—but from presence.
Not from striving—but from alignment.
Not from scarcity—but from enoughness.

May you remember:
You are not behind.
You are not incomplete.
You are already whole.

And from that place—
may you choose

a rich life.

Author's Note

THE WORK BENEATH THE WORDS

This book was not born
from theory. It was carved
from the inside out.

Every page was shaped
by questions I have
wrestled with. Choices
I have postponed.
Successes that felt hollow.
And moments—quiet,
humbling, sometimes
painful—when I
finally stopped long
enough to listen.

I wrote *The Fulfillment Curve* not as an expert looking down, but as a traveler walking beside you. Not to hand you answers, but to offer a framework, a mirror, a pause. Something to hold onto in the moments when achievement feels empty and alignment feels far away.

If there is one truth I hope you carry forward, it is this:

You are not broken.

You are not behind.

You are not defined by how fast you climb or how perfectly you perform.

You are the architect of your own becoming.

And fulfillment—real, grounded, durable fulfillment—is not something you earn by doing more. It is something you access by becoming more yourself.

So
keep
choosing.

Even when the world rewards the chase.
Even when it is easier to drift.
Even when it is messy, inconve-
nient, or misunderstood.

Choose stillness over spectacle.
Presence over performance.
Truth over trend.
The inside over the image.

Because that is where the rich life
lives—not at the top of the curve, but
in every return to what matters.

Thank you for walking this curve with me.

—Bill

www.ingramcontent.com/pod-product-compliance
Lightning Source LLC
Chambersburg PA
CBHW070027100426
42740CB00013B/2611